THE
LAWS
OF THE
SUN

IRH PRESS

THE
LAWS
OF THE
SUN

ONE SOURCE, ONE PLANET, ONE PEOPLE

EL CANTARE

RYUHO OKAWA

IRH PRESS

IRH PRESS
New York

ISBN 13: 978-1-942125-43-3
ISBN 10: 1-942125-43-7

Printed in Canada

First Edition
Fifth Printing
(2023 Revision)

Cover Designer: Whitney Cookman

TABLE OF CONTENTS

CHAPTER THREE
THE GREAT RIVER OF LOVE

CHAPTER FOUR
THE ULTIMATE OF ENLIGHTENMENT

CHAPTER FIVE
THE GOLDEN AGES

CHAPTER SIX
THE PATH TO EL CANTARE

Preface

It was in September 1986 when I wrote the first edition of *The Laws of the Sun* (published by Tsuchiya Shoten), so it has now been almost eight years since that time. This first book of my teachings sold millions of copies in total in both hardback and paperback and became a bestseller, making my name and the presence of Happy Science widely known throughout Japan. The English version of this book has also attracted many eager readers in places such as New York, London, Cairo, Sri Lanka, Tibet, and Sydney.

While I love and cherish the first edition very much, on this occasion, I have decided to make a more thorough revision and republish the new version through IRH Press. One of the reasons for this is that my enlightenment has advanced greatly during the last eight years. Another reason is that, at the time I wrote the first edition, Happy Science did not yet exist or have a single follower, but it has now grown into one of the largest religions in Japan.

I have spent dozens of hours thoroughly investigating the Spirit World to write this new edition and made significant revisions based on newly discovered facts. Also, I rewrote my personal history, putting in as much detail and writing it as objectively as possible (Chapter Six). I wrote it simply and straightforwardly because it seems that some Japanese journalists and religious scholars did not understand that I was trying to be humble in the first edition.

The Laws of the Sun is an exceedingly mystical book. Instead of trying to understand it using common sense, I want you to replace the usually accepted common sense with the contents of this book. Very soon, far more than 40 million avid readers of my books (hundreds of millions worldwide as of 2023) will make this book the common sense of the world. I hope it will be so.

Ryuho Okawa
Master and CEO of Happy Science Group
June 1994

CHAPTER ONE

WHEN THE SUN RISES

1

The Sun of Buddha's Truth

There is the term, *Buddha's Truth*. Buddha's Truth is the Mind of Buddha, the Rules of Buddha, or the Life of Buddha that is ever-changing. Further, Buddha's Truth is like a golden thread that weaves through the past, present, and future of humankind.

This golden thread called *Buddha's Truth* has been woven into various kinds of clothing throughout human history to protect people's minds from the cold. This clothing was once the teachings of Shakyamuni Buddha of India and, at another time, the teachings of Confucius of China. On yet another occasion, it was the teachings of love taught by Jesus Christ of Israel.

This clothing, which served to protect people's minds from the cold, was not only woven two or three thousand years ago; various types of clothing, large and small, have continually been sent to the world, from millennia past to the present day. In Buddhism, noble priests like Nagarjuna of India and Tientai Chih-i of China are famous examples. In Japan, the Buddhism that flourished under Kukai during the Heian period (794 - 1185) and the Buddhism that was revived during the Kamakura period (1185 - 1333) under monks like Honen, Shinran, Eisai, Dogen, Myoe, Nichiren, and Ippen were also forms of clothing of *Buddha's Truth*. The same is true with the restoration of True Pure Land Buddhism under Rennyo during the Muromachi period (1333 – 1573). In Japan today, the fifth religious boom[1] has arrived with the emergence of Happy Science and the greatest type of clothing of Buddha's Truth is about to be woven.

Buddha has thus been keeping people's minds warm by providing many clothes of various colors in order to protect them from materialistic and live-for-the-moment ideas that claim we only live once. To put it another way, Buddha is the great benefactor who has shone the Sun, called *Buddha's Truth*, so that people will constantly be given warmth and light for their minds. This Sun of Buddha's Truth has always and constantly been supplying the infinite energy of light to humankind. Indeed, it has been shining ever so brilliantly in the sky.

Certainly, there have been times when it seemed like this Sun of Buddha's Truth had disappeared from people's sight and remained inert, just as there are times when clouds block the sun, rain falls on people, and cold winds make them shiver. Far above the thick sea of clouds, however, the sun is always there, firmly radiating its golden light. Therefore, even if at times people's minds are confused and deluded, making it seem as though the light of Buddha's Truth has vanished from this world, a ray of the light of Buddha's Truth will always shine through. This very ray is the light of salvation; it is the light to save the world, the light of life to save people from times of darkness.

The Laws of the Sun that I am about to preach describes with truthful words how the Sun of Buddha's Truth, which seemed to have set, is rising again over the distant horizon after more than two thousand years. This time, it is rising as a far bigger sphere of light to give hope to the people of today and leave behind a golden treasure for future generations.

From this time on, as the Sun of Buddha's Truth rises, a great light will burst out from one corner of the globe. That particular corner is where Buddha has been reborn— Japan. Starting in Japan, many people will witness the Sun of Buddha's Truth rising brilliantly and gracefully. The world needs light now. There is a pressing need for Buddha's Truth to be spread with overwhelming power to crush the fortress of darkness named delusion, which humanity has long been working to build.

I am writing *The Laws of the Sun* in the hope that as many people as possible rise to spread Buddha's Truth as their lifework. I am writing it out, word by word, with a sincere prayer to save the world. I am writing this book as I pray that every single word in it will become a word of life, a word of light, to be cherished by all our brothers and sisters on Earth.

2

What Is Buddha?

You are currently living in this third dimensional world on earth, but have you ever given serious thought to the true meaning of your life? If you have, what are your conclusions? In considering life, we must first begin by defining it. Do you think life is just the decades of time spent in this world from one's birth till one's death? If so, then this book will completely overturn your views on life after just a few pages.

If life were finite and if you, an individual with a name that was given you by your parents, become nothing when you die, leaving behind just a handful of ashes and some bones after being cremated, with all else vanishing into the air as carbon dioxide and water vapor, then why do you bother to put so much effort into living your life? Why do you study and go through hardships? Why have you been deepening your understanding of life or pursuing your dreams?

Gautama Siddhartha—Shakyamuni Buddha—gave his teachings (Dharma) in India more than 2,500 years ago, but were they just complete lies? In his 80 years of life, he taught the meaning and mission of life, and the existence of the other world, or the Real World,[2] but were those doctrines just nonsense to delude people? Of course not. They were not doctrines made up by some uncivilized person.

Let me ask those who are proud of being modern intellectuals: who among you could ever master the Truth and expound it in a way that was so superior that it would be enough to refute the teachings of Shakyamuni Buddha? If you insist that the teachings of Shakyamuni Buddha are complete fiction, then what about the Truth taught by Jesus Christ 2,000 years ago? Can you claim that his teachings were equally non-sensical? More than a billion people in the world admire Jesus Christ, who had kept believing in God. But can you just dismiss God as a total fabrication based on Jesus' own personal belief and prejudice? Jesus was a true envoy of the Truth who prayed as he sweat blood in the garden of Gethsemane and was crucified wearing a crown of thorns. If you can call him a madman, you should come forward and prove to the world that you are sane.

To those who think of themselves as scientific and rational people, and say they will only believe in the existence of spirits after they see them, I say this: speak those words only after you have fully shown your deepest respect toward great figures like Shakyamuni and Christ, who have been honored for thousands of years of human history. If you are confident enough to laugh away the doctrines of those two, who have ceaselessly earned respect for millennia, you should prove yourself to be someone of greater integrity first.

No one can actually do such a thing because there is no one who has ever mastered Buddha's Truth more deeply than Shakyamuni Buddha, who achieved the highest level of enlightenment, or Jesus Christ, who was guided by El Cantare, the core consciousness of Shakyamuni Buddha.

Therefore, you must first be open-minded and start learning what Buddha's teachings are. This spirit is the exploration of scientific evidence in the truest sense.

As we explore life, we will inevitably encounter Buddha's guidance at some point. The opportunities to get to know Buddha's teachings are scattered everywhere in life. The moments of birth and death are the greatest opportunities, but Buddha shows glimpses of His very being at other times as well, such as when you are ill, in love, or are suffering setbacks.

Throughout this entire book, I intend to answer the question, "What is Buddha?" As I do so, I will also present you with many clues and answers on the purpose and mission of life.

3

Being and Time

We humans have seen all kinds of life and other things under the bright and shining sun from the time we were born into this world. In them, we must discover one Truth, a universal rule; it is the law of constant change. Everything that exists in this world is subject to this law of constant change, be it human, animal, plant, mineral, or microbe.

So, what is this law of constant change? It is the law that says that everything in this world passes through the stages of birth, growth, decline, and death. You can see an example of this in humans; there is the moment of birth, the process of growing into adults, the process of aging, and eventually, the time of death.

This law applies to all *things*, natural and man-made. Take, for example, a car. There is the time when the car is manufactured and the period when it is used efficiently for transportation. But it eventually starts breaking down and is finally scrapped. The same is true with plants; when a seed is sown, it buds, grows and flowers. But after it blooms, it will start to wither and eventually vanish, leaving behind nothing but seeds or bulbs. Thus, everything that exists in this third dimensional world passes through four stages: birth—growth or full operation—decline or disorder—death or dismantling.

In other words, all beings in this phenomenal world of the third dimension contain within them time for transformation.

Simply put, nothing can remain as it is. Everything is allowed to *exist* based on the precondition that it goes through change. We can also say that beings of this world, which are set to be in constant change, are like films being shown on a screen through a projector called time. In fact, all beings contain this characteristic of constant change: time.

If I were to explain this more simply, it means that every *thing* in this world is changing every moment; it is impossible to stay exactly the same. Even the cells in our body today are different from the cells we had yesterday. Although the human body is made up of cells that are changing every day, there is still substance with a name—a real live being that unifies the body's cells.

In essence, behind all beings, which are constantly changing in the flow of time, lies *something* that never changes. This is true with humans, animals and plants. For example, what makes a flower a flower is not its plant cells that came together at random. If the flower was just a random cluster of plant cells, then under the law of constant change, the flower would change into something else. However, a flower is always a flower: it was a flower yesterday, it is today, and it will be tomorrow. Only the stage of its growth will change; it will never become something other than a flower, such as an animal or a human. Likewise, a chrysanthemum never turns into a tulip, or a tulip into a cosmos flower. A tulip will end its life as a tulip, nothing else.

Within change is *something* that does not change; within constant change is *something* that never changes. This *something* is sometimes called *reality*, or sometimes *idea*. A well-known Buddhist expression, "matter is void—void is matter," are words of Truth that proclaim what I have just described: the ever-changing beings of this world are the projected images of the never-changing beings or universal beings that lie behind the change.

Human beings are not merely transient clusters of cells that constantly change with time. The true nature of humans is not an ephemeral being that changes in the flow of time, but an eternally unchanging being. This never-changing being is our very life, soul and spirit. By *spirit*, I don't mean some peculiar mysterious phenomenon; it is the very essence of human beings, the never-changing being, or the idea of life. Intelligence with unique character that governs the human body, and individual consciousness that keeps the physical body alive—these comprise the essence of human beings. Regardless of people's impressions about the word spirit, there is only one truth: flowers have life form as flowers, and humans as humans.

4

The Finite and the Infinite

So, I have just talked about time and explained being. Now, I would like to move on to the matter of what lies beyond time and space, that is, I would like to talk about the finite and the infinite. Is life finite or infinite? Is the universe finite or infinite? These are questions we all think about at least once.

Before drawing any conclusions, let me tell you a story. Once upon a time, there was a huge turtle. It took him 10 minutes to move his right foreleg, 10 minutes to move his left foreleg, and 10 minutes for each of his hind legs, meaning it took him 40 minutes just to take a step forward. One day, this turtle wondered if there was an end to the beach and decided to explore the world. Staring hard at the shoreline stretching far ahead of him, he began to move forward with all his might.

Taking as long as 40 minutes for each step, the turtle measured the shoreline. He left his footprints along the shore, so he could see where he had walked. He figured that he would not have to walk over the same place twice if he did this. You might think he was quite a clever turtle. However, no matter how far he walked, the beach was endless, and one day the turtle died of exhaustion. He died believing he must have explored at least half the world.

The following day, a fisherman came along and dragged the turtle to the other side of the island and ate it. Did it take a tremendous amount of time for him to reach the other side of the island? No, it took him just 10 minutes to walk there on his own sturdy legs. The poor turtle had actually been walking round and round the seashore of a tiny island, never noticing that the waves of the Pacific had been mercilessly washing away his footprints.

This story comes to mind whenever I think about the topic of the finite and the infinite. What was the difference between the turtle and the fisherman? Their walking speed? Certainly. Their body size? Certainly. The difference in experience? You could say so. But the fundamental difference, I believe, lay in their level of awareness. The turtle's goal, effort and enthusiasm were praiseworthy, but this story is colored by pathos because there is a distinctive gap between someone who can understand the Truth and someone who cannot, or between someone who can learn the Truth and someone who cannot.

Now, how about if I were to replace the turtle with a materialistic person and the fisherman with someone who has mastered the Truth? Some people may get angry and insist that they are not turtles.

Do you believe that life is finite and only lasts 60 or 70 years? Do you believe that everything ends with death? Do you believe that the world is limited to what you can see with your own eyes, openly denying the world beyond your five senses? If so, then you are like the turtle that set out to explore the world; you are just walking around in circles in the same small world, relying on nothing but your own footprints. I have to say that these people are truly pitiful. On top of that, they are struggling to live their lives sweating heavily, going round and round on a tiny island, just like the turtle. That is why they seem somewhat pathetic.

We human beings, with eternal life, have in fact been in existence since the far distant past. We accumulate life training by being born into this world over and over again.

In terms of the Earth's spiritual field, the space in which human life forms are active is not limited to this third dimensional world on earth. We essentially live in the Real World, or the world spreading from the fourth, fifth, sixth, seventh, eighth, ninth, and up to the tenth dimension. We each reside in different harmonious worlds that correspond to the level of our minds. So, if you are wondering whether the universe is finite or infinite, I have to ask you, "Are you thinking about the third dimensional universe, or the multidimensional universe from the fourth dimension and higher?"

If I use an analogy of the human body to explain the universe, our third dimensional universe would be the unclothed body. The fourth dimensional universe would be an undergarment, the fifth dimension a shirt over it, and the sixth dimension a sweater. The seventh dimension would be a suit over the sweater, and the eighth dimension a coat that covers the entire body. The ninth dimension would be like a hat on the head. This is just an analogy, of course, but it represents the structure of the multidimensional universe well. In essence, the higher dimensions contain the lower ones. They are not completely different from the lower dimensions; but while they may seem similar, they have a higher purpose—this is what we call the higher dimensional universe.

5

The Multidimensional Universe

I just explained the structure of the multidimensional universe using the analogy of a human body and the clothing that covers it. But this is just an illustrative description, so let me now give you a more theoretical explanation. To begin with, what is a dimension? We often say that we are living in the third dimension, but what does this mean?

Dimension is a grand perspective that describes a specific world according to the number of elements that shape it. For instance, the first dimension is a world of a straight line composed of a chain of dots. So, if there were people living in the first dimension, they would only be able to distinguish themselves from others by their length. In other words, you would either be longer or shorter than others. Therefore, if two people were exactly the same length, no one would be able to tell them apart.

In comparison, the second dimensional world comes with length and width. Length and width together make up a plane. So, if there were people living in the second dimensional world, they would just be a flat surface with no thickness, like a flatfish. Therefore, beings with identical length and width that are exactly the same shape and size would be indistinguishable.

Then what about the third dimensional world, the world we live in now? This world is composed of length, width and height, and together these give physical shape and form. So, in the third dimension, unless two people are exactly the same height, length and width, and are the same shape from all angles, they are not identical. In this sense, distinguishing one person from another is more complex than in the second dimension.

In the fourth dimensional world, the element of time is added to length, width, and height. This means that, while things that exist in the same space also share the same time in the third dimension, this is not the case in the fourth dimension. When we meet someone here on earth and shake hands, both of us are present in the same moment on the same day of the same month in the same year, but that is not how things are in the fourth dimension. To put it simply, when two people are shaking hands in the fourth dimension, for example, it does not necessarily mean that they are from the same time period. Someone from the fourteenth century and someone from the twentieth century can shake hands in the same place. This would never happen in the third dimension, but it does happen in the fourth dimension. So, when you see a building in front of you in the fourth dimension, it is difficult to tell if it exists in the present, or if you are looking at the image of it from the past. Also, even if it was an image from the past, you could still touch and feel it as if it were real.

In the fourth dimensional world, each person's watch shows a different time. For this reason, if you meet a woman who was born in Japan's Heian period (794 - 1185) in the fourth dimension, she would appear just as young as she looked when in her twenties. The same can be said of the way prediction works. Something that is to occur in the future in the third dimension may appear in the fourth dimension as if it were happening right now.

In the fifth dimensional world, yet another element is added to length, width, height, and time: spirituality. These five elements make up the fifth dimensional world. So, when the spirits of the fifth dimension distinguish themselves from others, they base their judgment on their shape formed by length, width and height, the time period to which they belong, and their level of spiritual awareness. To have awakened to spirituality or to the truth that humans are not physical, material beings, is a requirement to live in this world. One's spirituality is mainly measured by goodness. Therefore, the fifth dimension is a world full of only good-hearted people.

In the sixth dimensional world, knowledge of the Truth is added to the five elements of length, width, height, time, and spirituality. So, to distinguish one spirit from another, the spirits in this world base their judgment on their shape, the time they belong to, their level of spiritual awareness, and the amount of their knowledge of the Truth. The requirements for living in the sixth dimension are being a moral, good-hearted person and to have acquired knowledge of Buddha's teachings. Of course, the amount of knowledge of the Truth varies from person to person, and this makes for different levels within the sixth dimension; everyone in this dimension believes the Truth without exception.

6

The Universe of the Higher Dimensions

Let me now explain the seventh dimension and higher. In the seventh dimension, the element of altruism is added to those elements of the sixth dimension: length, width, height, time, spirituality, and knowledge of the Truth. If I were to describe the beings in the Spirit World up to the sixth dimension from a neutral perspective, they live in a self-centered way, but I do not mean that in a bad way. Even in the sixth dimension, a highly advanced world, spirits are still striving to absorb the knowledge of the Truth for their own improvement. In other words, spirits who live in the dimensions up to the sixth dimension are still students and, from a broader perspective, are yet to become working adults. If we look at the spirits of the sixth dimension as university students, those in the fifth dimension would be high school students and those in the fourth dimension would be middle school students, while people in the third dimension would only be elementary school students.

Only after reaching the seventh dimension can you say that you have completed your education and have set off into the working world. So, the main concern of the spirits of this dimension is altruism; it is expressed as love in their minds, and as service in their deeds. For this reason, the spirits of the seventh dimension not only give love and are of service to each other, but are also active every day guiding the spirits of the sixth dimension and lower. They are especially active saving the spirits who have left their physical bodies and are lost in the fourth dimension. The spirits of the seventh dimension are also born into the third dimension in human form, putting a life of love and service into practice. Thus, various holy beings live in the seventh dimension.

In the eighth dimension, mercy is added to the seven elements of length, width, height, time, spirituality, knowledge of the Truth, and altruism. Mercy is the heart of giving. It is the heart of those in higher positions to keep giving without hesitation or discrimination—this is mercy. While the love of the seventh dimension can be called "love that gives," the eighth dimensional love is even higher; it can be described as "love that continuously gives" or "endless love."

Seventh dimensional love is the fruit of human endeavor; it is to share the love you have accumulated through your efforts. But eighth dimensional love is much like the sun, that is to say, inexhaustible. This is mercy. While seventh dimensional love is selective or different in depth depending on who you give love to, the love of the spirits of the eighth dimension is fair and selfless. It is free of discrimination based on human ways of thinking. Because they are the suppliers of endless love, they deserve to be true leaders.

In the ninth dimension, the element of universe is added to the eight components of length, width, height, time, spiritual awareness, knowledge of the Truth, altruism, and mercy. The spirits of the eighth dimension and lower live within the stratosphere surrounding the Earth, forming a multidimensional world as the Earth's spiritual field. In contrast, the ninth dimension is not confined to the Earth's system, but is also connected to the Spirit World of other clusters outside our solar system. This means that the spirits of the ninth dimension are guiding the Earth Spirit Group in line with the evolution of the great universe. Most of the deities, Primordial God and Buddha of the global religions are in this dimension. The ninth dimension is thus a place for those who are the source of the Laws.

What distinguishes one from the other in this dimension is the difference in the color of their light as the source of the Laws. This is the only way I can describe it. That is, there is only one set of Buddha's Laws, of course, but it comes in seven colors depending on the character of the ninth dimensional being who teaches it.

Above this ninth dimension lies the tenth dimension, the highest level of Earth Spirit Group. In this dimension, there is no human spirit who has been born into a physical body because there exist only *three consciousnesses* there. If I were to list the elements of the tenth dimension, they would be creation and evolution in addition to mercy of the eighth dimension and universe of the ninth dimension. Tenth dimensional beings have no difference in individual character like humans do; they just take on different roles to carry out creation and evolution.

The three consciousnesses of the tenth dimension are Grand Sun Consciousness, Moon Consciousness, and Earth Consciousness. Grand Sun Consciousness governs the positive aspect or the proactive will of all living creatures on Earth, including humans. Moon Consciousness governs the passive aspect or the graceful, feminine aspect. Earth Consciousness is the consciousness of the planet's life force and governs the creation of all things on Earth. The 4.6 billion-year-history of Earth has been unfolding through the work of these three consciousnesses.

As for dimensions regarding Earth, the tenth dimension is the highest, but for our solar system, there is an eleventh dimension. The element of the eleventh dimension is the mission of the solar system; the eleventh dimensional being is the life force or the spirit body of the sun itself. Beyond this lies the galactic consciousness of the twelfth dimension. This is an enormously grand spirit that governs the galactic plan, reigning over hundreds of thousands of eleventh dimensional stellar consciousnesses, like the spirit of the sun of our solar system (in contrast, tenth dimensional beings are called planetary consciousnesses).

This is the most I can explain to you using words that you can understand. The Primordial Buddha (Primordial God) of the great universe is most certainly the Being beyond the twentieth dimension.

7

The Birth of Life (1): The Birth of Stars

What happens to humans after death is mainly a topic of interest in the religious sense, while the mystery of the birth of life—how human beings and other living creatures came into being—is mainly a topic of interest in the scientific sense. So, let me now talk to you about the mystery of the birth of life, and by doing so, also prove that religious interest and scientific interest have the same ultimate goal.

To begin, it is said that the third dimensional universe, of which our planet Earth is a part, was created approximately 40 billion years ago. Given that the Buddha of the great universe (Fundamental God) is the Being of the twentieth dimension or higher, He has existed as a consciousness from hundreds of billions of years ago—or more precisely, from time immemorial. By about 100 billion years ago the Primordial Buddha had designed a plan for the creation of the third dimensional cosmic space and around 80 billion years ago He created, by His own will, an enormously grand spirit who would rule the third dimensional universe. This was the birth of the thirteenth dimensional consciousness, which was the very first spirit involved in the universe of which we are aware.

The thirteenth dimensional cosmic spirit was the projection of the Primordial Buddha's consciousness that had the mission of creating the great universe. Approximately 65 billion years ago this thirteenth dimensional cosmic spirit created the consciousnesses of twelfth dimensional nebulae, of which there are about two million. One of them is the consciousness of the Milky Way Galaxy to which our planet belongs.

About 60 billion years ago, these galactic consciousnesses of the twelfth dimension created the stellar consciousnesses of the eleventh dimension, thereby giving birth to eleventh dimensional space. Namely, the twelfth dimensional consciousness of the Milky Way Galaxy created the eleventh dimensional consciousness of our solar system.

Then, approximately 53 billion years ago, the creation of planetary consciousnesses began in the Milky Way Galaxy, mainly led by the stellar consciousnesses of the eleventh dimension. This gave birth to the tenth dimensional universe. In our solar system, the workings of the stellar consciousness of the eleventh dimension then gave birth to the consciousnesses of Mercury, Venus, Earth, Mars, Jupiter, Saturn and other planets in succession. The creation of these planetary consciousnesses was nearly complete by about 42 billion years ago.

Then about 40 billion years ago, an unusual event took place inside the consciousness of the thirteenth dimension's grand cosmic spirit. Phenomena similar to nuclear reactions of fusion and fission—huge cosmic firework-like phenomena—occurred one after another. This was the so-called Big Bang. As a result, like the internal organs of a human body, a third dimensional space formed within the thirteenth dimensional cosmic spirit. Of course, at that time space was nothing like the currently ordered cosmic space; it was as if a transparent jellyfish-like space shaped like a stomach suddenly appeared. To give more structure to this jellyfish-like space, the galactic consciousnesses of the twelfth dimension, the stellar consciousnesses of the eleventh dimension, and the planetary consciousnesses of the tenth dimension worked as a group to create the physical forms of planets, stars and galaxies, one after another, in the third dimensional cosmic space.

During the 40 billion years since the creation of the third dimensional cosmic space, the rate at which Creation progressed varied from galaxy to galaxy and from one star system to another. In the Milky Way Galaxy, our solar system emerged in the third dimensional space approximately 10 billion years ago. Mercury was born 7 billion years ago, Venus 6 billion years ago, and Earth about 4.6 billion years ago. That was how our planet came into existence. Planets are the first consciousnesses with life to come into existence.

8

The Birth of Life (2):
The Birth of Human Spirits and
Other Life Forms

It is unclear as to when the first human spirit in the great cosmic space was born. However, there is no doubt that, when the original form of the third dimensional cosmic space was created 40 billion years ago, followed by the creation of nebulae, galaxies, and star systems, life in the form of stars was created first and, based on them, various other lives were born. To make things simple, here I will focus on the birth of individual life centering around our solar system.

It was approximately 10 billion years ago when the sun appeared as a star in the third dimensional cosmic space. Next, Mercury was born 7 billion years ago. At that time, though, our solar system was still uninhabitable. The first life in it was born after the beautiful planet of Venus was created. Venus was created 6 billion years ago, and half a billion years later, or 5.5 billion years ago, it was decided that the ninth dimensional world would be formed in our solar system. Then, a grand spirit was created; one with a human character, advanced to the highest degree, more mobile than the tenth dimensional planetary consciousnesses and suitable for ruling the living creatures that would later be born on the planet. This first grand spirit of the ninth dimension, the personified form of the tenth dimensional consciousness of Venus, was called El Miore. He was the ruler of Venus.

The first experimental life forms that El Miore created on the third dimensional surface of Venus were half animal and half plant: the upper part of their bodies was like lilies, and the lower part had two legs like humans. The many leaves that grew on their backs supplied them with energy to live by photosynthesis. These life forms were highly self-sustaining and had a long life span.

Next, El Miore separated plants and animals and let them evolve separately for about 2 billion years. Both the plants and animals were different from those we currently see on Earth; those on Venus were filled with beauty and grace. The plants grew jewel-like flowers and had a heavenly fragrance, while the animals were elegant and some even had the ability of speech.

Eventually, El Miore created Venusians that resembled the human beings of Earth today. For over 1 billion years, He would create a variety of species and during that time hundreds and thousands of civilizations were built. The Venusians advanced to the point where they could even interact with other star clusters by traveling on spaceships.

In their final stage of evolution, Venusians looked much like modern Earthlings, but were far more intelligent, equivalent to having IQs over 300. Both men and women had heavenly appearances with pearl-like radiance. Venusian women, in particular, possessed such beauty that they would make the most beautiful women on Earth seem similar to apes. Thus, a Venusian utopia abundant with dreams, love, beauty, and intelligence was realized.

The Venusians had built the most advanced utopian society based on love, wisdom, self-reflection, and progress. When the entire planet was about to turn into a world of bodhisattvas, El Miore received the following will from the Primordial Buddha of the great universe.

"The experiment of the civilization on Venus has been a brilliant success beyond expectations. Now that a state of perfect harmony has been achieved, further progress will be difficult. A massive volcanic eruption is planned on Venus in the near future, and it will be difficult for advanced life forms to survive. Some of the Venusians should emigrate to the friendly planets in other star clusters and help them evolve. All the other advanced spirits should remain in the Venusian Spirit World for several hundred million years to later participate in the creation of a new spirit group on neighboring Earth. You will have to start from the very beginning again, but I want you to create a new utopia on Earth. Invite foreign souls from unknown star clusters, educate them, and contribute to the evolution of the Milky Way Galaxy."

Thus, the next challenge was Earth. When the Earth was born 4.6 billion years ago, the same time that the life experiment and civilizational development was taking place on Venus, the tenth dimensional consciousnesses of Earth were also thinking about giving birth to earthly lives. Using the preceding experiment on Venus as a reference, they considered creating a spirit group of lives on Earth with a greater emphasis on dynamic evolution because the Earth had a more favorable environment in which creatures could live.

Then, based on El Miore's idea, the three grand spirits of the tenth dimension—Grand Sun Consciousness, Moon Consciousness and Earth Consciousness—established two basic pillars regarding the activities of life on Earth. The first pillar was to allow many levels for the expression of life in this world. The second pillar was to keep the activities in this world short-term and to make it a principle that beings would reincarnate between the earthly world and the multidimensional world.

Based on the first pillar, organisms like amoebas and plankton were created on Earth approximately 3 billion years ago. They became the basis of animals. About 2.6 billion years ago, mold and other fungi were created, and they became the precursors of plants. Gradually, increasingly complex life forms were sent down to the surface of the Earth.

Based on the second pillar, the bottom tier of the Spirit World was created first, which later developed into the current fourth dimensional Astral Realm. At the time, though, it was not yet clearly distinguishable; only a misty veil-like spiritual field draped softly over the land. At that early stage, microbes and simple plants repeatedly reincarnated between this lower Spirit World and the earthly world.

Then, about 600 million years ago, the three planetary grand spirits of Earth saw that the time had finally come to create advanced life forms on Earth. They created a ninth dimensional Spirit World on Earth and invited El Miore from its predecessor, Venus. El Miore, the very first personified grand spirit on Earth, first transferred to Earth the spiritual life forms that He had created during the early stages on Venus, and from them He created advanced life—mainly mammals.

How did El Miore go about the task of creating advanced life? First, He created the consciousnesses of animals such as mice, rabbits, dogs and cats, based on their concept in the lower Spirit World. Then, He gave them form on earth, one after another. This is how advanced animals gradually flourished in this world and reincarnation began to work smoothly.

Then, at last, El Miore spoke with the consciousnesses of the tenth dimension and insisted that it was almost time to create humankind in the earthly world. Accordingly, approximately 400 million years ago, a plan was made to give birth to humankind on earth. Around that time, El Miore, the former ruler of Venus and the first ninth dimensional being of the Earth Spirit Group, changed His name to El Cantare, which means "the beautiful land of light, Earth." Around 2,500 years ago a part of El Cantare's consciousness was born with a physical body in India as Gautama Siddhartha, also known as Shakyamuni Buddha.

9

The Launch of Earth Spirit Group

El Cantare planned to establish Earth Spirit Group based on the following two pillars: first, to give human beings different levels of spiritual awareness so that they could progressively advance on a perpetual basis; second, to make the human lifespan of this world short and to have them reincarnate between the earthly world and the Spirit World.

Then, El Cantare began creating earthly human beings using the advanced Venusian spiritual beings. He amplified His light of mercy and wisdom, and created a massive sphere of light in the ninth dimension. Then, He sent the most highly developed Venusian human spirits into the sphere of light, gave them the power of regeneration, and eventually split the sphere into smaller bits of light. This is how He created hundreds of Earth-born guiding spirits of light in the eighth dimension and below in Front Heaven.

To give each spirit individuality, El Cantare summoned all the powers of the ninth dimension and materialized them into this world. At first, transparent mirage-like waves appeared on the surface of the Earth. They gradually became silhouettes that resembled human form and finally turned into physical bodies shimmering in white light. El Cantare was delighted by the beauty and excellence of His creations.

When the first human beings appeared out of thin air one after the other—five, then ten, then one hundred, then five hundred—El Cantare divided them into two groups. He bestowed the light of Venusian wisdom and courage on those to His right, and the light of Venusian elegance and grace on those to His left. This was how humankind was divided into men and women. These were human beings with highly evolved souls, who later became the high spirits of Greece or Buddhist tathagatas, bodhisattvas, or kannons.

As the number of their physical descendants multiplied over time, many of the former advanced Venusian spirits accumulated physical life experiences as Earthlings. When their number surpassed 770 million in this world, El Cantare considered giving these physical descendants of the advanced humankind He had created experience as leaders. To do so, He felt the need to have other living creatures more evolved than anthropoids to dwell on Earth, so that the descendants could teach and guide them. Thus, He decided to invite humanoid beings from other planets. Around this time, in order to design a migration plan from other planets, El Cantare invited to Earth other ninth dimensional consciousnesses Amor (Jesus Christ) from Sagittarius, Therabim (Confucius) from Cygnus and Moria from Cancer, and asked them for their ideas.

At that time, however, dinosaurs and other gigantic life forms were beginning to roam around, and there was a risk that the newly arrived migrants unaccustomed to living on Earth could be killed. For this reason, the first humanoids invited were from planets in the Magellanic Clouds, a rather self-assertive, egocentric, and combative type of race. Having possessed highly advanced technology, they came to Earth on spacecraft.

Physically, they closely resembled people of today, but they had the unique characteristics of pointed ears and feline tails. These features gradually diminished over time, but due to the self-image they retained deep in their minds, some of them transformed into *tengus* (goblins), *sennins* (hermits), ogres, monsters, and the like, even after they returned to the heavenly world.

The advanced human beings of El Cantare's spirit group, as the royal family or royal leaders of Earth, implemented plans to help the migrants become assimilated to the life on Earth. However, although the leaders among the migrants possessed large amounts of light energy, some of them started to behave like selfish and vengeful gods and disturbed the planet's harmony, so they were sealed into Rear Heaven. This is how Front Heaven and Rear Heaven were formed in the sixth, seventh, and eighth dimensions of the heavenly world.

One of the leaders of this Rear Heaven is a being we now call Enlil (a ninth dimensional spirit in charge of Rear Heaven). Afterward, some 120 million years ago, one of Enlil's direct subordinates, Lucifel, was born on earth with the name Satan, but he lost himself to the worldly status, fame, material possessions, and sensual pleasures, and thus became corrupt. Unable to return to the higher Spirit World, he formed the world of Hell in the lowest part of the Spirit World and started a revolt. He then became the king of Hell with the name Lucifer.

Because the migrants from the Magellanic Clouds were egocentric and had few harmonious qualities, El Cantare decided to invite another human race to Earth. As a result, 270 million years ago, as many as one billion beings from the constellation

Orion came to Earth in an enormous fleet of space ships. This marked the second migration from outer space. By this time, there were already 10 billion Venusian spirits from El Cantare's spirit group going through reincarnations on Earth, so there was accommodation in place to take in such a massive number of immigrants.

This was also when three other ninth dimensional grand spirits came to Earth, namely, Achemene, Orgon, and Kaitron. Achemene is a high spirit called Manu, known in Indian mythology as the "progenitor of humanity." Orgon, also known as Maitreya Tathagata, was very active during the age of Ramudia and Atlantis, but has rarely incarnated on earth during the last ten thousand years. Kaitron, known in theosophy as Koot Hoomi, in charge of the development of science and technology, was born in Greece as Archimedes, and later on as Isaac Newton.

This occasion was taken as a good opportunity to establish and enlarge the fifth dimensional Goodness Realm of Earth, so that it could take in greater numbers of spirit groups. Then approximately 150 million years ago, the core consciousness of El Cantare descended to this world and built an enormous civilization of light. Buddha's Truth for Earth was established and the training of migrants from other planets progressed greatly. The number of people who devoted themselves to El Cantare kept increasing one by one, which created a common mindset among the people on Earth.

Furthermore, 130 million years ago, in commemoration of El Cantare's spirit group surpassing 40 billion individual spirits through the repeated branching off of light in the high Spirit World, a third massive migration took place, and approximately two billion beings from the constellation Pegasus came to Earth. At this time, Theoria and Samatria, the ninth and tenth spirits of the ninth dimension, respectively, came to Earth. Theoria was born in Greece as Zeus some three thousand years ago. Samatria was born twice in the area of Iran. He was known as Zoroaster and Mani, and is the founder of Zoroastrianism and Manichaeism.

This was how the ten grand spirits had gathered in the ninth dimension and established a governing system for Earth Spirit Group. Around this time, the role of the fourth dimensional Astral Realm for the new Earthlings was becoming clearer.

10

The Increase in Spirits on Earth and the First Fallen Ones

As described earlier, by approximately 130 million years ago, the El Cantare Spirit Group had exceeded 40 billion spirits, while the population of migrant spirits had expanded to more than three billion. Around this time, Enlil and some others suggested that the number of human spirits from other stars should be increased significantly. Enlil proposed using relatively advanced spirits among those that migrated to Earth as a core from which to produce five branch spirits. According to Enlil's idea, if these spirits each took turns experiencing earthly lives, it would be more efficient in terms of learning. So, a gigantic device called the Pytron was created; the Pytron amplified the light of higher dimensions, and by shining it at a core spirit, it would thereby give birth to five branch spirits.

However, the creation of human spirits with the Pytron was banned after several hundred million human spirits were created, due to the spiritual levels of many of these branch spirits it produced being inferior. As they experienced earthly lives, an increasing number of them forgot that they were essentially spirits, becoming corrupt by clinging to material things and physical desires, and exerting bad influences on other good spirits. After death, these human spirits began to form a spiritual field of their own in the lower realms of the Spirit World. Then, spirits with dark thoughts formed a group in the fourth dimensional Astral Realm. This was the beginning of Hell.

The Pytron was the second mistake Enlil had made, the first mistake being the disharmony created by Enlil's group of migrant spirits from the Magellanic Clouds. So once again, he received strict guidance from El Cantare. What is worse, when Lucifer organized the rebellion against the high spirits of the heavenly world and established Hell 120 million years ago, the negative thought energy of the spirits in Hell formed dark clouds that prevented Buddha's light from entering their world ever again. So, Hell became a cold, dark place.

Further, this created a problem in the third dimension; the dark world which was formed in one area of the fourth dimension began to block Buddha's light from shining onto some areas of the third dimension. No matter how brightly the sun might be shining, clouds in the sky can cover it and form shadows on the ground. Likewise, starting 120 million years ago, all kinds of evil and chaos began occurring in the third dimensional earthly world.

From then on, a conflict has continued for over 100 million years, mainly in the third dimensional phenomenal world. Tathagatas and bodhisattvas of higher dimensions have been trying to purify the earthly world, while the devils and evil spirits of Hell, led by Lucifer, have been desperately making counter-efforts to expand their territory in the third dimension to escape their agonies in Hell. This is why El Cantare has sent His own branch spirits to the third dimension many times and built up a powerful guidance system to train guiding spirits of light through the power of enlightenment.

I am writing *The Laws of the Sun*, so that the light of Buddha can shine once again, that is, for the Sun of Buddha's Truth to regain its brilliance in the third dimensional earthly world. I hope you will understand deeply the history of the Earth Spirit Group that I have explained in this chapter and imagine how seriously and earnestly I will be preaching the Laws. *The Laws of the Sun* teaches the laws of salvation to rebuild Buddhaland, the original world of light.

ENDNOTES

1 Since the emergence of Happy Science, the fifth religious boom has been observed in Japan on a completely different level than that of former booms of new religions. (Also, there has not been any particular growth in the number of followers of religious groups other than Happy Science. In addition, a clear distinction must be made between groups that have caused social problems, such as Aum Shinrikyo and the Unification Church, and the leading religion Happy Science.) The fifth religious boom refers to the rise of a spiritual movement to completely change the atheistic, materialistic climate of Japanese postwar society and, at the same time, implies the emergence of an advanced religion that provides clear guidelines for creating a new civilization in future society.

Going beyond the framework of Japan's new religions, Happy Science is now on the path to become the fourth world religion after Buddhism, Christianity, and Islam. A vast surge is already beginning to form to integrate these three world religions, surpass them, and establish Buddha's Truth on a global scale.

On a side note, the first religious boom took place in Japan between the end of the Edo period and the beginning of the Meiji period, when new religions such as Kurozumikyo, Konkokyo and Tenrikyo were active. The second boom came with new religions such as Omotokyo, which thrived in the Taisho period and in the beginning of the Showa period. The third boom took place after Japan's defeat in World War II, when an abundance of new religions appeared: this period is sometimes called "the rush hour of the gods." The fourth boom occurred in the 1970s when Japan's rapidly growing economy slowed down, causing people to feel insecure, and pollution problems surfaced. Psychic religions, including GLA, Mahikari, and Agonshu became very popular. Although the popularity of the revival of the age of spirituality gained momentum, it also created all kinds of misguided religious groups, making a religious revolution by Happy Science inevitable.

2 Shakyamuni Buddha's acknowledgement of the existence of the Real World is clearly stated in many of his teachings. For example: in the stories of brahma pleading with him to preach the Truth and his battle with the devil (Agama Sutras); in the "Step-by-Step Teaching," which teaches that accumulating spiritual virtues through making offerings and following the precepts will allow you to be reborn into Heaven; in the concept of the twelve links of causality in relation to our past, present, and future lives (see Part One, Chapter One of *The Challenge of Enlightenment*, Sphere, 2006), which was not Shakyamuni Buddha's direct teaching but appeared in early Buddhism; in the teachings of nirvana and of void; in the tale of his descent into his mother's womb from Heaven in the form of a white elephant; in his sermon for his departed mother, Queen Maya in the Spirit World; in the promise of his disciples' attainment of Buddhahood in future lives (Lotus Sutra). Some Buddhist scholars unknowingly distort Shakyamuni Buddha's teaching of egolessness in a materialistic way, but they are destined for Hell for their mistakes and their misinterpretations must be dismissed altogether (see Part One, Chapter Four of *The Challenge of Enlightenment*, Sphere, 2006).

CHAPTER TWO

BUDDHA'S TRUTH SPEAKS

1

The Truth about the Soul

In Chapter One, I described the history of the creation of the universe and the formation of Earth Spirit Group. As you have read, Creation was a process in which higher-dimensional beings created lower-dimensional beings. To be more precise, the Will of the Primordial Buddha of ultra-high dimension created the higher grand spirits in each dimension, one after another. After stellar consciousnesses and planetary consciousnesses were born, an odd event occurred inside the grand spirit of the great universe, giving birth to the early form of the third dimensional universe. In time, stars were created in the third dimensional space, forming star clusters, and living space was created in each star system for spirits with human character of the ninth dimension and lower.

In our solar system, too, the spirit group on Earth started with the creation of the ninth dimensional Cosmic Realm. It was then followed by the eighth dimensional Tathagata Realm (Diamond Realm), the seventh dimensional Bodhisattva Realm (Divine Heavenly Realm), the sixth dimensional Light Realm[1], the fifth dimensional Goodness Realm[2], and the fourth dimensional Astral Realm (including the Fairy Realm and Hell), in that order. Similar multidimensional structures exist in other parts of the universe as well. But although the ninth dimensional world is connected to the Spirit World of each star cluster, the eighth dimension and lower develop independently, specific to the Spirit World of each planet.

This clearly shows that the life form of each individual, which we often call "soul," is a lower-level manifestation of the Primordial Buddha in a dimension far above. This means that the Primordial Buddha is not something that exists somewhere outside of you, but is a high-level consciousness that is at the base of your existence. In other words, you, too, are a part of Buddha's consciousness and self-expression.

Simply put, the Primordial Buddha created the great universe and all life forms that live in it as a part of His self-expression. Everything is the reflection of His Will. So, if He no longer wanted to maintain the great universe, then one day, this seemingly infinite third dimensional universe would vanish abruptly. This is also true with humans; if Buddha abandons His Will to express Himself, human life forms would disappear without a trace. Humans are such ephemeral beings. Yet, these ephemeral individual life forms are also high-level beings, as they are part of Buddha's consciousness.

Therefore, you should take pride and have confidence in the fact that you are a part of Buddha and are playing a part of His self-expression. This is the truth about the soul. Past religions and sophisticated philosophies have been developed and passed down in order to awaken people on earth to this truth. The ultimate purpose of natural science and space science, which are now making tremendous progress, is to reveal this truth about the soul.

Starting off with this wonderful truth concerning the soul, that you are part of the consciousness of great Buddha, I will now talk about how souls or human life forms should essentially be. I am sure what I talk about will reveal Buddha's Truth.

2

The Nature of the Soul

What, then, is the nature of the human life form, or the soul, which is a part of Buddha? It is by exploring the nature of your soul that you will be able to catch a glimpse of the nature and character of Buddha.

The soul has several distinctive qualities. The first quality is its creative nature. The soul has been given the ability to change itself however it wants by the use of its own will. In other words, it can decide for itself what kind of thoughts it bears as a consciousness. For example, a soul can choose to exhibit the highest level of love, or it can choose to exert the highest level of freedom. By choosing the kind of thoughts you hold in your mind, you can freely control the amount of light within you and elevate yourself to be a higher-dimensional being, or even reduce your light and be a lower-dimensional being.

Then, does this mean that it is part of the soul's nature to do evil, think evil, or be corrupt? Is falling to Hell, or forming Hell, also the work of the soul's creativity? The answer to these questions is both yes and no. It is "yes" because souls have been given the freedom to create, and freedom essentially means there are no restrictions or constraints. If there were restrictions or constraints, that would not be freedom. On the other hand, the answer is also "no" because the soul was not originally created to commit evil or to create Hell. Evil is not in the nature of the soul. Evil is simply a distortion or friction that arises when souls with freedom come into conflict with one another. Essentially, humans cannot commit any kind of evil when they are alone because evil can only arise when they come in contact with another person, another creature, or another object.

Since ancient times, the dualism of good and evil has been discussed in many ways. People's fundamental questions have been about the reason why evil exists in a world created by Buddha and whether evil is a hidden nature of Buddha Himself. But evil, of course, is not in His nature, or Buddha-nature. Evil is what obstructs the achievement of the Great Vow of Buddha. It is merely the friction or distortion that temporarily appears either in people's minds or in the phenomenal world as the result of a conflict between people's freedom, or a clash between people who have been given freedom by Buddha. This means that evil is not a primary existence in itself; it is an effect of a function or deed.

The second quality of the soul is its role or nature as the center that concentrates and disperses the light of Buddha. What, then, is Buddha's light? It is His energy that fills the great universe. Just as there is sunlight shining on the earthly world, there is heat energy that pours down brilliantly onto the multidimensional universe from the fourth dimension up to the higher dimensions. It is Buddha's light. No living organism in this earthly world can continue living without the thermal energy of the sun. In the same way, no life form in the fourth dimension and higher in the Real World can live without Buddha's light or Buddha's heat energy.

It is the soul's nature to be able to concentrate, absorb, emit, and amplify this light of Buddha. We consider those who can absorb and emit a large amount of Buddha's light as having plenty of light. They are the ones known as the guiding spirits of light. Tathagatas and bodhisattvas have a tremendous ability to concentrate and emanate Buddha's light and can send light into other people. In short, they are able to bring bright light into people's minds. All human souls live by absorbing and dispersing Buddha's light. But the high spirits that emanate Buddha's light, or guiding spirits of light (angels of light) including tathagatas and bodhisattvas, are able to supply the light of Buddha to other people; it is for the sake of illuminating the world and to fill people's minds with light.

If souls have the ability to concentrate and disperse Buddha's light, then what about the souls in Hell? For those souls, the supply of Buddha's light energy has been cut off. Actually, they are blocking Buddha's light with massive dark clouds of negative thought energy that they created themselves. So, they are living in dark, damp, cave-like places. They no longer live on Buddha's energy; the source of their energy is the negative thoughts harbored by people living on earth.

People in this earthly world absorb Buddha's light to make it their spiritual energy, but at the same time, they generate energy on their own from the food they eat and convert it into life energy. The spirits in Hell actually come to steal this self-generated energy. They plug into the dark clouded areas in the minds of people on earth and take away their energy from there. As they come to possess living people one by one, they take away their energy and vitality, ruining their lives. They are, in a way, vampires that suck the energy out of living people.

To prevent possession by such spirits of Hell, we must not allow them to plug into our minds. To do this, we must not create dark, damp areas in our minds that attune to the spirits of Hell. We simply must not create in our minds the "cancer cells" that block Buddha's light. Then, the spirits of Hell will no longer receive their supply of energy, and Hell will eventually disappear.

3

Embodiment of Buddha

What, then, are bodhisattvas of light? I would now like to focus on this issue. The word *angel* sounds Christian while *bodhisattva* has a Buddhist tone, but some tathagatas in Buddhism are also called archangels in Christianity and the word bodhisattva can also mean angel. As I have described earlier, both Buddhism and Christianity are essentially Buddha's Truth; they just differ in the color of light depending on the character of the religious founder. So, it is not a big difference whether we call high spirits "great guiding spirits of light" or "angels of light." That is, they should be considered embodiments of Buddha in the eyes of common souls or ordinary people.

All humans were created equal by Buddha, so why do such high spirits or embodiments of Buddha exist? Doesn't the very existence of these high spirits mean there is discrimination in human character to begin with? If that were the case, ordinary people would lead ordinary lives together and high-class people would lead high-class lives together, in separate groups.

Why are there high spirits as well as low spirits? I must answer this question from the standpoint that Buddha's worldview comprises two perspectives—equality and fairness.

All human beings, all animals, all plants, and all minerals have Buddha-nature dwelling within them. No matter how each is expressed outwardly, all things are manifestations of Buddha's

Will. This is Buddha's Truth, whether you believe it or not. To put it differently, each and every creature is made of diamond called Buddha's wisdom. Buddha implanted diamonds in many ways to make humans in one way and plants in another, thereby arranging vivid and beautiful art. Take any human, animal, or plant, it is made of Buddha's diamond called wisdom. This is the Truth.

Buddhism calls it "Buddha-nature" that is inherent in all creatures; it is an idea that considers humans children of Buddha. Therefore, everyone, be it a high spirit or a low spirit, is equal in that it embodies Buddha's life. In this respect, all beings are equal. Those who proclaim the difference as unequal are just misled by the words "high" and "low."

The fact is that there are highly developed spirits, developing spirits, and undeveloped spirits. All spirits are walking the same path, but the difference is that some are walking ahead while others are walking behind. The highly advanced guiding spirits of light were created a long time ago, so they have already walked a great distance and are therefore closer to reaching their destination, which is Buddhahood. On the other hand, most of the undeveloped spirits were created more recently, so they are naturally walking behind.

Can you say this is unequal? Is it discrimination to assess spirits based on the distance they have traveled? This is something to be evaluated from the standpoint of fairness, not of equality. Not all spirits necessarily go forward on the path, even if they have existed since ancient times. Some ancient souls go backward on the path. For example, spirits who were once angels can become devils in Hell. They had once advanced so far, but somehow made a wrong turn and went backward. They should be called regressed spirits rather than undeveloped spirits.

Buddha maintains equality by having all spirits travel the one path that leads to Him. Also, He maintains fairness by evaluating all spirits based on the distance they have traveled. This means that high spirits, or embodiments of Buddha, have made achievements worthy of their status and have been given appropriate roles accordingly. All spirits undergo eternal discipline to become like these high spirits.

4

The Structure of the Soul

I have talked about how there is a difference in development among human spirits, or souls, and explained the reason for this difference by introducing Buddha's points of view—equality and fairness. Next, I would like to move on to the structure of the soul. It is often said that a core spirit and branch spirits exist, or that the surface consciousness of a soul lives on earth in human form while the subconscious exists beyond in the Real World. To help you understand this more clearly, let me share my thoughts with you.

In the beginning, the Primordial Buddha that exists beyond the twentieth dimension created the consciousness of the grand cosmic spirit of the thirteenth dimension. This thirteenth dimensional spirit then created the galactic consciousnesses of the twelfth dimension, which then produced the stellar consciousnesses of the eleventh dimension. These stellar consciousnesses then created the planetary consciousnesses of the tenth dimension. Consciousnesses with human character begin to appear in the ninth dimension. These consciousnesses are the ninth dimensional grand spirits.

They are consciousnesses with distinct characteristics, but their entire energy bodies are too great to reside in the human body. Therefore, when they are born into a physical body in the third dimension, only a portion of their consciousness comes down. Gautama Siddhartha and Jesus Christ were parts of ninth dimensional grand spirits that were individualized and born into human bodies, becoming souls that represented the character of the grand spirit. In this way, the soul is essentially a spirit with a human character. When the souls of ninth dimensional beings leave their physical bodies and return to the ninth dimension, they will become a part of the grand spirits' memory. The number of souls into which ninth dimensional grand spirits are capable of splitting themselves is infinite in this meaning; they are completely free and have unrestrained capabilities.

The situation is somewhat different for the great guiding spirits of light in the eighth dimensional Tathagata Realm. They, also, are grand spirits, but are even more distinctive in their characters. An eighth dimensional spirit usually lives in the heavenly world as one integrated consciousness, but when necessary, it can divide itself into any number of spirits to carry out its work. For instance, Bhaisajyaguru Tathagata, the tathagata of medicine, has one integrated character as an eighth dimensional spirit, but when there is work needed in the field of medicine, this spirit can split into thousands or tens of thousands of spirits and begin to guide the people on earth or other spirits in various countries of the world. So, to carry out one specific purpose, an eighth dimensional spirit can divide into as many spirits as the job requires, while retaining itself as one integrated character. They differ in this point from the ninth dimensional grand spirits, who can take on different characters for multiple purposes while retaining a single nature of light.

Concerning the spirits of the seventh dimensional Bodhisattva Realm, they are more distinctly separate as individualized human spirits. Put differently, there are consciousnesses in the eighth dimension and higher in the heavenly world that have never been born into the earthly world, but every spirit in the seventh dimension has experienced human life on earth. The seventh dimensional spirits of the El Cantare spirit group place great importance on teamwork and, as a general rule, each group is comprised of six spirits. One of the six which takes on the central and leading role is called the "core spirit," while the other five are called the "branch spirits." These six spirits take turns coming down to earth and work as bodhisattvas. In principle, the one who is next in line to incarnate would take on the role of the guardian spirit, which is for its own preparation as well. But to cope with the complex structure of modern society, there are increasing cases in which the spirit that was most recently born on earth acts as the guardian spirit. Each spirit shares all of its experiences with the other five spirits, and they all have the same tendencies. Just as the human body is composed of six body parts—the torso, two arms, two legs, and the head—a spirit is made up of a group of six souls.

In the sixth dimensional Light Realm, however, the six spirits have little awareness as one being and each spirit is independent. So, they have difficulty understanding the concept of soul siblings, or of a core spirit and branch spirits. In the Light Realm and lower, there are spirits who were created about 100 million years ago by a giant device called the Pytron, which amplified and emitted the light of higher dimensions to produce five copies, or branch spirits, out of a core sixth dimensional spirit. But the spiritual levels of these branch spirits were slightly lower, so most of them became spirits of the fourth dimensional Astral Realm or the fifth dimensional Goodness Realm. Since there was a need for these human spirits to raise their spiritual level, they have come to reincarnate between this world and the other quite frequently for the last 100 million years.

In the sixth dimension and lower, the core spirit usually guards and guides its branch spirits when they are undergoing training on earth. However, if the original group of six has difficulty functioning properly as a result of a gap in awareness that came about because of different experiences on earth, there are situations where members of the group are switched with the power of Buddha's light.

5

How the System of Guardian Spirit and Guiding Spirit Works

In the world of religion, people often use the terms *guardian spirit* and *guiding spirit*. Let me now explain these terms, beginning with guardian spirit. People often believe that they have a guardian spirit watching over them, and that if it is powerful, their lives will improve, but if it is powerless, they will experience misfortune. The answer is, guardian spirits do exist, and are assigned one per person. It is also somewhat true that a person's life is affected depending on the abilities of his or her guardian spirit. So, I will reveal the secret why guardian spirits began to protect people living in this world from the other world, namely the Real World.

More than 300 million years ago, when highly advanced human beings of the El Cantare spirit group first began to live on earth, they did not have guardian spirits. But since people's hearts were pure, they were able to communicate directly with the spirits in the Real World. In those days, Hell did not exist and there were no evil spirits, so there was no need to assign guardian spirits to protect humans from negative spiritual influences.

However, about 120 million years ago, spirits with disharmonious thoughts began to gather in the fourth dimensional Astral Realm, the bottom part of the heavenly world, and formed the dark world of Hell. Since they could no longer receive the energy of Buddha's light, they brought confusion to the earthly world and made people produce thought energy such as desire, evil, and disharmony in order to feed on that energy. This was something completely unexpected. The spirits in Hell crept into the minds of people on earth, caused them to have negative feelings such as disharmony, conflict, anger, jealousy and make complaints, as they plotted to fill the world with distrust and confusion.

Therefore, the guiding spirits of light in the heavenly world urgently met to determine how to deal with the situation. At that time, the following three guidelines were decided as proposed by Amor, the one currently known as Jesus Christ:

1. In principle, humans on earth will no longer be allowed to communicate directly with the Spirit World in order to prevent evil spirits from taking complete control of them. Instead, they will be encouraged to choose ways to make their lives better in the material world.

2. Everyone will be assigned a guardian spirit upon his or her birth on earth for protection from the temptations of Hell.

3. Great guiding spirits of light will be sent to earth periodically to give religious teachings and inform people of the Real World in order to prevent people from completely forgetting about it.

These three basic principles have been observed for more than 100 million years. But since Hell grew quite large, it became very difficult for a single guardian spirit to fully protect a person undergoing soul training on earth, just by its powers alone. What is more, common people who are not religious leaders were prohibited from directly communicating with the Spirit World, so they could no longer recall memories of their past lives. Ironically, they became even more caught up in worldly, materialistic desires.

Further, conflicts between different religions and sects began as byproducts of guiding spirits of light establishing new religions on earth in different periods. Devils and satanic spirits of Hell took advantage of this and crept into the minds of religious leaders as well, causing them to preach mistaken teachings. This created further confusion in the earthly world.

With this backdrop, naturally, it was of great significance and urgency for us to spread Buddha's Truth. But above all else, the system of guardian spirits needed to be revised. In basic principle, a guardian spirit is either a spirit of its own soul group that had split off from Buddha's light in the Spirit World, or a spirit of a group of six created as core and branch spirits. However, it was determined that when a person who is to be born has an important mission and is expected to accomplish it at all costs, that person will be provided with a guiding spirit that has the same specialty as that person's major career in life. Especially, religious leaders are assigned to have as their guiding spirits, tathagatas or bodhisattvas who are more powerful and higher in spiritual grade than they actually are. The system of guardian and guiding spirits was firmly established in this way. Nonetheless, it seems that people living on earth are continuously having their destinies manipulated by various evil spirits.

6

Evolution of the Soul

Due to the influence of Hell, earth has been put into great disorder and confusion for the past 100 million years. However, this is not to say that the whole of the Earth Spirit Group is degenerating. In the long run, on the contrary, many spirits have been making steady progress, which is remarkable. This is what the evolution of the soul is all about.

There are souls that have evolved considerably even among those that were created on Earth. Some distinguished souls have advanced successively as they kept reincarnating and went from the fourth dimension to the fifth, from the fifth to the sixth, and from the sixth to the seventh. So, there are Earth-born spirits that have developed to the same level of the high spirits who had originally come from other planets, becoming high spirits themselves. There has not yet been any spirit created on Earth that has evolved to the level of the ninth dimensional Cosmic Realm, but some have reached the eighth dimensional Tathagata Realm, giving great joy to the spirits of higher dimensions. This was actually the true purpose of forming the Earth Spirit Group in the first place. What this means is that the high hopes they had when immigrating to Earth, to make it so harmonious and advanced, much more than the planets they had come from, are beginning to be realized.

Today, there are nearly 500 tathagatas in the eighth dimensional Tathagata Realm, while there are about 19,000 bodhisattvas in the seventh dimensional Bodhisattva Realm. Of these, there are 130 spirits who became eighth dimensional tathagatas for the first time on Earth, and about 7,000 who reached the seventh dimensional Bodhisattva Realm. Even among the new souls created through the Pytron, a number of them have also managed to progress to the upper part of the sixth dimension and become various gods, as well as those who have become bodhisattvas in the seventh dimension. Contrary to the bad news of the expansion of Hell, there are also such good reports.

So, then, why are souls expected to evolve? How can they actually do so? I would like to answer these questions now.

Firstly, why do souls evolve? To answer this, we need to trace back to the fundamental reason and begin from there. In other words, before considering why souls need to evolve, it is essential to consider the reasons why Buddha created souls of different levels in the first place. If evolving to a higher degree were the only purpose, then there would have been no need for Buddha, Himself, who is already the most evolved Being, to create souls of lower dimensions and have them evolve. This would not be completely logical, either.

The reason why Buddha created consciousnesses and souls of different levels and allowed them to develop is because He appreciates the byproduct that comes with evolution, not just the evolution itself. For example, if parents are already complete individuals as they are, then why do they need to go through all the effort of having and raising children? They do so, not for the sole purpose to have their children become fully developed adults, but because the very act of giving birth to children and raising them is accompanied by joy. Through raising children, families will not only be more joyful, there will also be happiness.

In the same way, Buddha created consciousnesses and souls of different levels and wishes for their evolution and progress because the very process of their evolution is accompanied by great joy. In other words, by the creation of the great universe and the creation of each life form aiming to evolve further, all would become the expression of Buddha's joy and the source of His happiness. This is the fundamental reason why the principles of evolution exist in the great universe. Buddha is watching over, with boundlessly kind love, the consciousnesses and souls He created, as they continuously strive to become like Him by evolving, progressing, and improving themselves.

Next, let me explain how souls can evolve. One indication of how much a soul has evolved is by the amount of light it has. In the Real World, we can clearly see the level of a soul's growth by looking at the amount of light it has. The same is true of the people on earth; as they advance in their spiritual training and progress in their enlightenment, the amount of light they have gradually increases and what is known as an aura forms at the back of their heads. Those with spiritual sight will easily know a person's stage of enlightenment by looking at his or her aura.

The auras of people whose minds are attuned to Hell are dark and hazy, with whitish spots here and there. Since these white spots sometimes wiggle, it is easy to tell what areas are possessed. Those whose minds are connected to the fourth dimensional Astral Realm (Fairy Realm) have small auras of just one or two centimeters (half an inch) emanating from the back of their heads and from their entire body. Those whose minds are attuned to the fifth dimensional Goodness Realm have auras of about three to four centimeters (1.5 inches) at the back of their heads. Those whose minds are connected to the sixth dimensional Light Realm have yet larger auras that are rounded and extend about 10 centimeters (4 inches). Those whose minds are attuned to the level of arhats or of various gods from the upper part of the sixth dimension have small, circular tray-like auras that are shining gold. Those whose minds are attuned to the seventh dimensional Bodhisattva Realm have golden ring-like auras of 40 or 50 centimeters (about 1.5 feet) in diameter above their shoulders. And those whose minds are connected to the eighth dimensional Tathagata Realm emit light of one to two meters (3 to 6 feet) in diameter around them that very gently makes their surroundings brighter.

In this way, the extent of the soul's evolution is shown by the amount of light it has. Simply put, in order to make your soul evolve, you need to enlarge your capacity to receive more and more of Buddha's light. To do so, you must make sure that you do not create dark clouds in your mind that block His light. You must devote yourself to accumulating spiritual training to expand your soul's capacity.

7

The Relationship Between the Mind and the Soul

In this section, I would like to move on to the topic of the mind and the soul. So far, I have used the terms *consciousness*, *spirit*, and *soul*. Although these terms are not necessarily used in the strict sense, you can assume that human attributes get stronger in the order of consciousness, spirit and soul.

Are the soul and the mind the same thing? Let me expound on this. The conclusion will be that the mind is the core part of the soul. The soul is shaped like a human body, and, just as the heart lies at the center of the human body, the soul has a central part called the mind. The mind is located neither in the head nor in the brain cortex or cells. As proof of this, we retain all memory of our lives, even after we die and return to the other world. When the physical body is lost, the cerebral tissues naturally disappear from this world. After they are cremated, they vanish into the air as carbon dioxide and other things. However, the soul can still think, feel, and remember even without the brain.

The brain is a file cabinet or an information control room where all kinds of information are organized. So, when this brain or information control room is damaged, we can no longer judge or act rationally because the entire command system of the physical body falls into disarray. Suppose a man is mentally impaired due to a brain injury. Although his family may think that he is incapable of understanding any of their words, this is actually not true. He can understand everything they say despite his mental disorder. In fact, he understands everything in his mind, or through the central part of his soul. He is just showing unusual behavior because he cannot express that he understands. So, even if he is mentally ill due to his physical disorder while he is alive, he can think and act just like those who led sound lives when he dies and returns to the other world.

If the mind is not in the brain, then you might think it is located in the heart. It is certainly true that the soul often recognizes the mind to be located near the heart, but the heart mainly controls blood circulation, and is not the mind itself. Yet, as people have been saying since older times, our hearts begin to race when we are in panic, our hearts ache under the weight of grief, and our hearts nearly stop when we experience great fear. When we are happy, we feel warmth come from somewhere near our hearts and when we are sad, we feel tears well up from somewhere near there, too. From this, we can see that although the heart is not the mind itself, it is an organ that is closely related to the mind and susceptible to spiritual influences.

If we imagine the soul to be shaped like the human body, the primary center of the mind is located around the chest, and mainly controls the will, emotions, and instincts. Moreover, intellect and reason give commands to the entire soul through the secondary center of the soul, located in the brain which is like the outpost of the mind. Further, one's spiritual intuition is directly connected to one's soul siblings in Heaven in the Spirit World through the lower belly, heart and brain. A spirit is essentially energy without a fixed shape, but by dwelling in a human body, it becomes a soul, or a body of thought shaped like a human. The spirit undergoes life training with the mind situated at the center of the soul.

People leading their daily lives on earth often deny the existence of spirits or souls without a second thought, but they probably cannot deny the existence of the mind so easily. Even those who materialistically believe that the mind is located in the cerebral cortex will shed tears when they are sad, but this is not after the brain decides that they must do so. When we feel sad, sadness wells up from our hearts in an instant and tears begin to flow. This is only natural. When we meet an old friend unexpectedly, something warm wells up from our hearts and we spontaneously hug that person. These are not reactions of the cerebrum, but reactions of the mind based on our spiritual intuition. Cerebralism, which states that everything can be explained as functions of the brain, is another form of materialism, so we must clearly deny it. I will continue to speak more on this wonder of the mind from here on.

8

The Workings of the Mind

Human beings are consciousnesses, spirits, and souls that Buddha created with His Will. I have already talked about this truth many times. I have also explained that the mind is the core part, or the most crucial part, of the soul. Now, I would like to explore the mind in further detail focusing on its workings or functions.

It is often said that our thoughts can be transmitted to other people. For example, when you like someone, that person will sense your feelings even though you don't show them, and will gradually begin to like you as well. This actually happens often. The opposite is also true. When you dislike someone, that person will also sense your feelings even though you don't show them and the relationship between the two of you will become uneasy. Then, how is this kind of telepathic communication— where thoughts are transmitted from mind to mind—possible, and how does it actually happen? Let me consider this point.

The workings of the mind actually include the creative power that Buddha gave to human beings. Buddha created the different dimensions with His Will. He created the third dimensional universe, the souls of humans, as well as their physical bodies. Each and every human being is a part of Buddha's consciousness, and by itself is a complete single miniature universe. Therefore, the workings of the human mind originate from His creative power and are similar to it. So, every thought and feeling creates something somewhere in this third dimensional universe and in corresponding multidimensional space. Further, the collection of the thoughts of all individuals becomes the power that creates the Real World.

That being said, there are different levels or strengths of thinking: thoughts, concepts and will. First, thoughts are things that come up in our minds at various moments in the day and can be said to be a part of our usual mental activity. Second, concepts are thoughts that are more concrete. While thoughts are like the daily ebb and flow of waves at the seashore, concepts are somewhat continuous and include detailed vision; they can be visualized as pictures or video images. They have a story line and, like the water of a flowing river, have continuity and direction. Third, there is the will. It has a distinctively creative nature; it even possesses a physical force. In the fourth dimension and higher, the will creates all sorts of things as it has a creative power similar to that of Buddha.

Even in the third dimensional world, the mental function of the will has great physical power. For example, if your will is focused on the wish to guide someone in a positive direction, a sudden change can actually happen in that person's mental state or circumstances, making a turn for the better. If, on the other hand, you have an intense dislike for someone, and this hatred becomes stronger and more focused until it becomes your will, then the recipient might fall ill, experience various misfortunes, or even die early.

A similar effect occurs in large groups. If hundreds of thousands or millions of people strongly wish to make this world a Buddhaland utopia and their will is gathered and amplified, light will shine from that part of the world. The light will penetrate into people's hearts, spreading their world of happiness even more. In this way, the earthly world can turn into a world of bodhisattvas. Of course, the opposite scenario is also possible. What would happen if this world were filled with people's negative thoughts, such as hatred, anger, and selfishness? Seen with a spiritual eye, negative thought energy would look like dark thunderclouds forming and floating over different parts of the world. This body of thoughts would then turn into physical power to cause yet greater confusion on earth.

As we have seen, the workings of the human mind are wonderful, but at the same time dangerous. This is why we need to do a thorough self-reflection to see how our minds are working.

9

The Mind Can Attune to
Three Thousand Worlds

Our thinking becomes more powerful as it progresses up the order of thought, concept, and will. Now, I would like to take this idea a step further and explain the concept, "the mind can attune to three thousand worlds."[3] This notion was often referred to by the Chinese monk, Tientai Chih-i (538 – 597). More than a thousand years ago, in the Tientai Mountains in China, when Chih-i taught this concept, it was actually my own spiritual consciousness who was guiding him from Heaven in the Spirit World. The following is the contemporary interpretation of the message I sent to Tientai Chih-i in the Tientai Mountains from the world of the ninth dimension, during the sixth century.

"Within the minds of humans is a compass needle, which is their thoughts. This needle swings constantly and points in various directions all day long, with no rest. Even the needle in the mind of monks who have devoted their lives to spiritual discipline swings when they see young beautiful women. The needle moves when they see a delicious meal. It also swings when they see others awaken sooner than they do. Moreover, the needle moves when their master admonishes them. The minds of seekers know no peace.

"But true enlightenment of humans is attained within great harmony and peace, not in a constantly turbulent mind. Tientai

Chih-i, you must attain a high level of enlightenment and clearly indicate to people the direction in which the needle in their mind should point. Humans will never attain peace of mind as long as their needle of thoughts keeps moving. The needle of the mind should always point in the direction of Buddha, just as a compass needle always points north. Just as the North Star indicates north, Tientai Chih-i, you must teach and guide people well, so that they can live with the Will of Buddha as their own. This is what it means to have true unshakable mind and true faith.

"The mind is truly a wonder. If your mind is focused on battle, it will attune to the Ashura Realm in Hell (the Hell of Strife) and you will unknowingly lead a life of strife and destruction. If the needle of your mind steadily points toward sexual pleasure, your thoughts will be connected to the Hell of Lust, and the spirits of Hell will use the needle to trespass into your mind. As a result, you will obsess over the opposite sex and end up as a tool for those spirits to satisfy their lust. If the needle of the mind of those who seek Buddha becomes distorted at some point and they become conceited and arrogant, they will start to preach false or wrong teachings and mistake the voices of devils for the voices of tathagatas and bodhisattvas. Some pitiful seekers mislead people and end up falling into Abysmal Hell themselves.

"On the other hand, there are also people whose minds are always filled with good thoughts, with the needle of their minds pointed to the Goodness Realm of the fifth dimension in Heaven.

Their friends and ancestors in Heaven are always watching over them with a smile. There are also others who devote themselves to helping others, remain humble and modest, and continue to seek the path to Buddha. Their minds are attuned to the Bodhisattva Realm in Heaven and are in a bodhisattva state although they are still alive in this world. There are yet others whose needle of the mind is set on spreading the Truth. They give the right teachings, have noble character, and live in a way that can serve as a good model for all people. Their minds are already attuned to the Tathagata Realm although they are still alive. They receive constant guidance from tathagatas in the heavenly world.

"In this way, the needle of the mind works in wondrous ways. Tientai Chih-i, you must deepen your understanding of this Law and help others with their spiritual training as they live their lives.

"Heaven and Hell exist not only in the other world, but they also exist here in this world. They exist in your mind. The needle of your mind can point in all directions and, depending on your thoughts, it can immediately point to Heaven or to Hell. Once people become aware of this Truth, they will want to set aside some time every day to enter a meditative state, calm their minds, reflect on their lives, look back on their day, and correct their wrong thoughts and actions.

"Tientai Chih-i, the Eightfold Path that I taught in India was based on this law of the mind that I have just now revealed to you: the mind can attune to three thousand worlds. Heaven and Hell do not exist only in the world after death, but also in the minds of people living in this world; the thoughts you have while you are alive in this world will directly determine the way you will live in the other world. This is exactly why human beings must live with the Eightfold Path as the basis of their life.

"The Eightfold Path consists of seeing rightly (Right View), thinking rightly (Right Thought), speaking rightly (Right Speech), acting rightly (Right Action), living rightly (Right Living), making efforts rightly (Right Effort), concentrating your will rightly (Right Will), and entering meditation rightly (Right Meditation). Only when people have mastered these eight paths can they maintain the right state of mind and reach human perfection. Tientai Chih-i, correct your mind and deeds based on these eight paths, and spread this true teaching, 'the mind can attune to three thousand worlds.' This is your enlightenment and the enlightenment for the people of the world."

10

The True Eightfold Path

So far, I have talked about the concept, "the mind can attune to three thousand worlds," and about the Eightfold Path. To conclude this chapter, I would like to explain the significance of the Eightfold Path in the context of modern life.

Human beings are spiritually blindfolded. While they are alive, they just search for ways to survive based solely on information gained through the five senses, and often remain unaware of the world that exists beyond those senses. The truth, however, is that the true meaning of life lies beyond the five senses. Although this may seem paradoxical, our five senses can help us awaken to what lies beyond them. This being so, let us not simply lament that we are blind to the true life. Instead, blind as we are, why not discover the truth by feeling our way carefully, that is, by sharpening our five senses? In this very effort, the True Eightfold Path will reveal its nature.

The Eightfold Path is the path to human perfection; it is the wisdom to correct our misdirection and to lead the right life. There is no model answer as to how you should live your life. That is because life is a series of questions and each of these questions differs depending on the circumstances you are in, the experience and knowledge you have gained, and the habits you have acquired. You yourself are the one who must solve these questions, not someone else. You are the one straying off the path. Who in the world will correct your course, if not you? That is why each and every person must explore even deeper what is right within the framework of his or her own life.

What, then, is the standard for this righteousness? What defines righteousness? Answering this question is the mission of true religious leaders and it is my mission in this lifetime.

To know what is right is to know the Mind of Buddha, to scientifically explore His life. What is good and what is evil? What is true and what is false? What is beautiful and what is ugly? Buddha's Mind determines the answers to these questions. To know Buddha's Mind is to investigate the nature of the body of energy of His light. In short, to know Buddha's Mind is to make the utmost effort to understand Buddha.

In addition to *The Laws of the Sun*, I have been writing other books on the theory of the Truth to help you deepen your understanding of Buddha's Mind, or the nature of Buddha's body of energy. These teachings will be the greatest keys for you to learn the Mind of Buddha. I hope you will learn the Mind of Buddha, grasp what is right, and use that as your guide to practice the Eightfold Path. The Buddha's Truth that I am telling you is authentic; your minds will be shaken and tears of self-reflection will certainly well up when you read them, as long as you are not under the influence of devils or evil spirits. You should live with the righteousness that I teach as a guideline for your life. As you do, I hope you will live every day using each of the following points as material for self-reflection.

1. Did you look at things rightly the way they are, based on right faith? Did you observe others rightly? Did you treat others as Buddha would treat them? Did you humbly accept a true perspective of life and the world? (Right View)

2. Did you think rightly? Is your aspiration for enlightenment appropriate? Did you harbor any negative thought in your mind, such as greed, anger, or discontent? Did you think badly of others, or bear malice toward them? Did you become arrogant or doubt Buddha's Truth? Did you have any thoughts that went against Buddha's Truth? Did you make right judgments? (Right Thought)

3. Did you speak rightly? Did you say anything that bothers your conscience? Did you hurt others by using abusive words? Did you lie about the level of your enlightenment? Did you use flattery to mislead others and make them conceited, or distress others by speaking in a way that created distrust among them?
(Right Speech)

4. Did you act rightly? Did you violate any of the precepts of truth seekers? Did you use your hands, your legs, or any other part of your physical body to commit any crimes, such as murder, assault, or theft, as well as to

commit any sexually immoral acts, such as extramarital affairs, sexual abuse, engaging in the sex industry, or indulging pornography? Did you respect the lives of all living creatures? Did you make generous and sincere offerings to the Three Treasures of Buddha, Dharma, and Sangha? (Right Action)

5. Did you live rightly, keeping your actions, speech, and thoughts in harmony? Did you live in an unhealthy way, overindulging yourself in alcohol, tobacco, gambling, or drugs? Did you have any complaints about your life, or did you know how to be content? Did you give thanks for all things? Did you make full use of the twenty-four hours that Buddha gave you? (Right Living)

6. Are you studying Buddha's Truth in the right way? Are you losing the will to train yourself spiritually? Just how much were you able to keep yourself away from doing evil and plant seeds of goodness? Do you make a constant effort to improve yourself? (Right Effort)

7. Are you able to calm your mind and sustain a right life plan in terms of your soul training and the creation of Utopia? Are your prayers for self-realization in accordance with the Mind of Buddha, and do they help raise the level of your enlightenment and further refine your character? Do you have a deep understanding of

Buddha's Truth? Do you remember the teachings of the Truth correctly? (Right Will)

8. Do you regularly take time to concentrate your mind rightly? Have you reflected on the sins you've committed in the past? At the end of the day, do you look back over your day thoroughly and offer gratitude toward your guardian and guiding spirits? Have you managed to attain peace of mind by concentrating your mind? (Right Meditation)

The above eight make up the True Eightfold Path[4], which has not lost any of its value even today. It is the right way to live as a human being. Correcting yourself each day in this way will create an extraordinary life, and this very effort will become the power to elevate you toward the heights of Buddha.

ENDNOTES

1   In the early days of Happy Science, I used the term *"Shin-kai* (Godly Realm)" to refer to the sixth dimension, but not all gods of Japanese Shinto belong to the sixth dimension; actually, there are many who belong to the eighth dimensional Tathagata Realm and the seventh dimensional Bodhisattva Realm. Therefore, to avoid misunderstanding, I will use the term "Light Realm" from now on.

2   For the fifth dimension, too, I used to use the term "Spiritual Realm" in a narrow sense, but in a broader term, it also means the vast world that extends from the fourth dimension to the ninth dimension and above. Since the spirits in the fifth dimension are characterized by their good-hearted nature, I will use the term "Goodness Realm" from now on.

3   According to Chih-i's teaching, all existences can express themselves according to the following Ten Factors: 1) appearance (outward look); 2) nature (inherent nature); 3) entity (main traits that make up a being); 4) energy (potential abilities); 5) influence (outward functions); 6) internal cause (direct cause that triggers an event); 7) conditions (complementary cause); 8) effect (brought about from cause and condition); 9) reward (brought about from effect) and 10) consistency from beginning to end (factors from one to nine are all consistent and interrelated).

   There is also the teaching on the Ten Worlds—the realms of Hell, Hunger, Animality, Strife, Humanity, Heaven, Hearer, Solitary Realizer, Bodhisattvahood, and Buddhahood—each containing the other nine realms. Everyone originally belongs to one of these realms in the Spirit World and, while living in this world, people's minds can attune to any of these ten realms at any given time. Ten types of people can express ten types of minds—so effectively, there are one hundred types of minds altogether. When these one hundred types of minds are multiplied by the above ten factors of existence, we get a total of one thousand worlds.

   What's more, there are three Realms of Existence: 1) Realm of Living Beings: individual living beings; 2) Realm of Five Components: an individual consists of matter, feelings, perception, volition, and consciousness; and 3) Realm of Environment. When multiplying these variations, the total number of worlds is three thousand. Realm here is defined as a different time and space.

   This is a brief summary of the theory behind the concept, "the mind can attune to three thousand worlds" (refer to Chih-i's works, *Hokkegengi* ["The Essentials of the Lotus Sutra"] and *Makashikan* ["Mahayana Practice of Calming and Contemplation"]). This philosophy is very abstract and Chinese-like, but simply put, it means that the human mind can be expressed in three thousand ways, illustrating the ever-changing nature and the limitless possibility of the human mind.

4   In this section, I have explained the Eightfold Path in the same order as originally taught by Shakyamuni Buddha, but I have introduced a different approach in my other books, from a practical point of view.

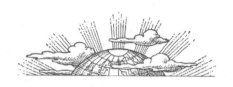

CHAPTER THREE

THE GREAT RIVER OF LOVE

1

What Is Love?

In this chapter, let us think about love. Love is probably the topic that you are interested in the most; you may think of it as the most important matter. Love is, no doubt, the most important and brightest thing that human beings experience in the course of their lives. People are often captivated by the word *love*, by the very sound of it. It inspires us with dreams; it makes us passionate; it inspires us to seek adventure.

Suppose today is the last day of your life. Although you are destined to die this evening, if someone offers you words of love, each one of you would be able to depart this world with a blissful smile. A life without love is like an exhausting journey across the desert. A life with love is a life with oases filled with flowers here and there located in the desert.

Looking deeper, what is love? Who, if any, has succeeded in defining love accurately? Writers? Poets? Philosophers? Perhaps, after all, religious leaders?

How much can you understand love? How deeply can you observe its true nature? This is one of the challenges, or problems, given to humankind. At the same time, love brings us joy and happiness, as well as distress and suffering.

Love is extreme in two ways. True love leads us to the greatest happiness, while false love leads us to the deepest unhappiness. Love makes up the majority of joy in life, but if misunderstood, love can cause the majority of life's distresses. Grasp the essence of love and apply it freely as you wish, all while aiming to attain the greatest happiness—it may seem as though a ray of bright light shines in that way. It may seem as though God is waiting for you somewhere on that path, smiling with open arms.

Anyhow, in this chapter, I will contemplate the essence of love, its stages, the relationship between love and enlightenment, and finally, God and love.

Oftentimes, I have had discussions with Jesus Christ, who resides in the heavenly world, regarding love. As you may know, Jesus Christ is a great master of love, an expert on love, and an embodiment of God's love. Such a figure has said that it is so very necessary to teach what true love is to the people of today. Apparently, he said, this is because throughout history, love has rarely been as misunderstood as it is today, the only other eras being the end of Atlantis and the age of Sodom and Gomorrah described in the Old Testament.

Nevertheless, I would like to face this topic of love squarely and answer the questions that the people of today have. Practicing the Eightfold Path and exploring love—this is the desirable form of spiritual discipline for modern people, and should be a gospel for them as well. So, from here on, I will try to tell you much about love. My words should provide you with views on life, the world, and the Truth, from the perspective of love.

2

Love Exists

People have many opportunities to think about love, yet no one has ever seen it. This is because you cannot hold love in your hands or take it out and show it to others. However, love is something that definitely exists. Humans believe in the existence of love. They set out on an eternal journey without destination to seek for the existence of love—some proof that everyone can confirm to be love.

No one has ever seen love; no one has ever touched love. Is it nothing more than just a fantasy, an illusion? But consider this: how many invisible or intangible things do people believe in? Take the wind, for instance. You cannot confirm the existence of the wind with your own eyes, yet you believe that it exists as you see leaves whirling up in the air or hear the trees rustling. You know the gentleness, coldness and strength of the wind because it caresses your skin. You can describe the wind in these ways, but you cannot capture it, put it in a box, and take it out to show others.

Love is like the wind. Everyone believes and shares the feeling that love exists, yet no one can objectively prove it. You cannot prove that love exists, but you can feel its presence. Although you cannot take hold of love and call it love, you can sense that it is there.

Oh, how similar love is to God.[1] Countless people have spoken about God and believed in Him, but no one has ever been able to bring Him to show to others that He is God. So many great figures in history have talked so much about God in the forms of religious teachings, philosophy, poetry, or literature, yet no one has been able to provide proof regarding the existence of God. Even Jesus Christ could not show people what God looks like. He could not show people and say, "Look here. He is God, the Heavenly Father."

Jesus frequently told his followers, "Anyone who hears me hears my Father in Heaven. It is the Father who is now speaking through me. Anyone who sees my work sees the work of my Father in Heaven. It is the Father who is doing His work through me." Jesus often taught people to perceive God through his words and actions. People, after listening to Jesus' words of authority, sensed God in him and became devoted to him.

Ironically, the most important things for human beings are often the hardest to prove. This will always be true. In any age, it is more often the case that the most important things cannot be proved. God, love, courage, wisdom, goodness, kindness, beauty, harmony, advancement, mercy, Truth, sincerity, selflessness—the universe is rich with all these realities. There is not a being in the world of light who does not know these words. In the earthly world, however, not a single person can prove that these are real because these precious values all belong to the Real World in the fourth dimension and higher. That is to say, these things cannot be proven using the materials of the third dimension.

The Primordial Buddha (Fundamental God) whom I now recognize is the Being of extremely high dimension beyond the twentieth, so it is impossible to prove His existence based on third dimensional standards. This is why there is faith. To have faith means "to believe and worship"; to believe means to feel and accept, whereas to worship means to respect something greater and to humble oneself.

"God is love."[2] Jesus said so. Love is undoubtedly one of the attributes of God, but Jesus meant something more.

"God's existence is not meant to be proven. However, if I were asked what resembles God, it is love. No one can prove that love exists, yet people know its wonderfulness and the goodness it can bring. They strive to attain love, and they believe in the power of love.

"Such is faith. Those who believe that love exists shall believe that God exists. Those who believe in the power of love shall believe in the power of God, for God is love. Behold—I, Jesus Christ, the son of God, do the work of love. Yet, it is not I performing these deeds, but my Heavenly Father, my God, who descends to me and makes me do such work. If you wish to see love, then first, see the work of mine. In it there is love, and in it there is God."

The above words are the resurrection of the sermon on love that Jesus Christ gave in the land of Nazareth about 2,000 years ago. At the time, I was the one who was guiding Jesus from the heavenly world. That is why I know his words.

3

The Power of Love

As far as I know, love has the greatest power in this world. Love is the greatest power in the Real World as well, the world also known as the multidimensional world of the fourth dimension and higher. What is more, as you go higher up the dimensions, the power of love becomes stronger. This is because love is the power to connect to one another. While the power of excluding one another weakens each other, the power to connect will make a person's power twice or three times as strong. Therefore, love has no enemies; where love goes, no enemy stands in the way.

Love is a shielded chariot. Love is an armored vehicle that travels over hills and down valleys, that crosses rivers and swamps, and that effortlessly breaks through fortresses of evil.

Love is light. Love is the light that shines through the dark night and illuminates the past, the present, and the future. Love is the light that shines in Heaven and on earth, as well as upon people's minds and hearts. Love is the light that can even dissolve all evil in this world with infinite gentleness, and embrace all sorrow of this world with infinite warmth.

Love is life. All people live on the food called love; they live with love as their power; it is their flame of life. That is because love is everything. Without love, there is no life; without love, there is no death. Without love, there is no path; without love, there is no hope. Love is all and everything; it is our food, our life.

Love is passion. Passion is the power of youth and the belief in infinite possibility. Within this very intense energy are something true and the inexhaustible vigor of life.

Love is courage. Without love, people cannot rise to action; without love, people cannot confront death. Love is the torch that lights the fuse of Truth; love is the arrow shot at delusion.

Love is a vow. In the name of love, people live together, speak to one another, and walk together. Without the bond called love, people will lose their way and only wait for the sun to set.

Love is words. Without words, there is no love; without love, there are no words. Love is good words, good thoughts, good vibrations, and good melodies. With words, God creates the world; with words, love nurtures people.

Love is harmony. Only with love do people cherish each other, forgive each other, nurture each other, and create a wonderful world. In the circle of love, there is no anger, no envy, and no jealousy; in the circle of love, there is only great harmony where everyone nurtures one another.

Love is joy. Without love, there is no true joy; without love, there is no true happiness. Love is the expression of God's joy and the magic that sweeps away all sorrow in this world. Love is joy, which gives birth to more love, and this love produces more joy. In this way, love is circular; it is a cycle.

Love is advancement. One love leads to one advancement; one love produces one light. Days with love are days of advancement, for where love goes, there is God; for where love goes, there are countless holy spirits. Where there is love, there is no regression; where there is love, there is no fear. Love only advances; love only improves. To love means to fly toward God, nothing more.

Love is eternal. Love is in the past, present, and future. There has been no time without love; in every age there have always been people with love. Love flies across all time with its shining golden wings. Love is Pegasus that gallops across the heavenly skies far above. Love is the proof that lives through eternal time; love is the hunter who captures the eternal moment of now.

Finally, love is prayer. Without love, there is no prayer; without prayer, there is no love. Through prayer, the power of love becomes more proactive. Through prayer, love achieves all things. Prayer is the power to elevate love; prayer is the sacred rite that will deepen love. Thus, by praying to God, love achieves itself; by praying to God, love manifests itself.

God is love and love is God. Prayer is the power to have love work as God. Through prayer, people live; through prayer, people come to know God. In this way through prayer, people can exert the power of love to its fullest.

4

The Wonder of Love

Love is truly a wonder. Its profoundness and height cannot be measured. The more we think about love, the deeper and richer it seems. God, rather than reveal Himself to humans, probably sent love to earth on His behalf. By having humans learn about love, God must be helping them understand what He is truly like, and gives them material for their own learning. The wonder of love is this: it makes us feel the presence of an invisible power. This is why love is a wonder.

Now, let me tell you a parable about the wonder of love. Once upon a time, there lived an old man, all alone and with no children or grandchildren. He lived in a small temple on the outskirts of a village where local children would sometimes come to play. The naughtiest of them all was Taro, a thirteen-year-old boy who had lost both his parents at an early age and was being raised by his older sister and her husband.

One day, Taro was playing on the steps that led up to the temple when three sparrows flew down. They landed right next to where he was sitting and began to converse.

The first sparrow said, "The most important thing in this world is the sun. Thanks to the sun always shining in the sky, we can enjoy the different colors of nature; the trees and flowers take delight. The crops grow rich and we sparrows can benefit from them, too. If the sun were ever to hide, the world would become dark and no creature would be able to live. We sparrows are always grateful for the sun, and we would never take the lives of fellow sparrows. But as the sun is always shining gently, humans become arrogant and do whatever they want; they fight and quarrel among themselves. Some are even foolish enough to engage in war. Someday, the sun might get so disappointed that it will hide itself."

Hearing this, the second sparrow spoke. "To be honest, water is the most important thing in this world. Without water, nothing can live. Without water, the trees and plants would begin to wither in a week. Rice and wheat would not grow either and we would all die. Animals could not last a week without water. We owe our lives to water, so I believe water is the most important in this world. We sparrows are grateful for water, so we live in harmony. But foolish humans do not value water because they believe it is free. They would rather work hard to obtain useless jewels or necklaces. We sparrows are content with how God made us at birth, but humans are so concerned with making themselves look good. It is truly ridiculous what they are asking for—to attain a higher position than others, to be richer than others, or to be more beautiful than others."

Then, the third sparrow finally spoke saying, "Sun and water are certainly important, just as both of you said. The most precious things in this world seem to be what everyone takes for granted, things so natural that everyone does not even realize them. Everyone is not aware of this, but in my opinion, the most important thing is the air. Even if the sun were to disappear and the water to dry up, we would still be able to live for a few days. However, if there were no air, we would die in less than a minute. We do not realize how much of a blessing it is until we are told. We sparrows are grateful for the air we fill our lungs with when we fly through in the sky. Even the fish in water are thankful for the air as they come up to the surface to take a breath when they need to. Oh, how arrogant human beings are in contrast to that. They believe they can fly on airplanes thanks to their cleverness. But this is not right. Their airplanes can fly because there is the air. The air does not ask for anything, not even a penny, whether we fly or humans ride in their airplanes. We sparrows are grateful for the air, but I've never seen humans be thankful for the air."

On hearing the conversation of the three sparrows, Taro felt truly sad and fell into deep thought. He had been taught that humans were the lords of creation and the greatest of all, but he had not heard anything like the sparrows' comments. He had never thanked the sun, water, or air. How foolish and ignorant humans were! They were inferior to sparrows!

With those thoughts, Taro arose quickly and went up the steps. Surprised by his sudden movement, the three startled sparrows flew off. Taro met the old man who lived in the temple and told him the story he had just heard. As he began to weep, he told the old man that if humans were so foolish, he wished he had been born a sparrow rather than a human.

Then the old man replied, "Taro, you have learned well. Humans are so foolish that they have lost sight of the most important things in the world. Even so, we are forgiven our sins by loving each other. Humans indeed lack sense, but no matter how much we focus on our negative traits, they will not go away. God has given humans the magical power of love to forgive our sins and wipe away our foolishness. With this wonder of love, humans are allowed to remain the lords of all creation."

5

Love Has No Enemies

Love is the greatest power, love is without enemy. Thus, I would like to talk about how love is invincible. Human beings encounter various adversities in the course of their lives. I mean, humans undergo soul training as they live their lives. This actually has been predetermined. What are these difficulties? They are, simply put, illness, poverty, and setbacks. Also included are heartbreaks, business failures, broken friendships, and separation from loved ones. One may also encounter someone one dislikes. Furthermore, people grow old, lose their looks, lose the ability of their body control and functions, and eventually die.

If we look at these phenomena only as they appear, life may seem to be filled with distress and sorrow. However, there is a meaning to our distress and sorrow; they urge us to make a choice. By choice, I mean that each one of us must choose between a life of giving or one of being given.

The essence of love is in giving. To love is to share what God has given to us with others, rather than just keeping it ourselves. The love of God is infinite. No matter how much love we give to others, there is no limit because God has been supplying us with love.

The essence of love is, first and foremost, to give. Please understand this point well.

Those who are suffering from love, listen well. Why do you suffer? Why do you suffer from love? Why do you suffer by giving love to others? Do not expect anything in return. Expecting something in return is not true love. True love is love that gives. Love that gives is unconditional love. The love you give is not yours to begin with; your love is the love given to you by God. We should love other people in order to return this love to God.

The cause of your suffering lies in the belief that, although you love someone, he or she does not love you. No, it is not that the other person does not love you. You might think you are not loved as much as you had hoped. That is why people become distressed by love. But the reward for your love comes not from other people, but from God.

What is the reward that comes from God? It is that the more you give love, the more you become like God. That is the reward from God. Look at the true nature of God. He provides infinite love and mercy to all creatures without asking for anything in return, just as the sun showers its light brightly onto us. Even the life of each and every one of you is the energy given to you by God, and this did not cost you anything.

This being so, start off by giving. Giving means to live every day thinking of ways to make as many people as possible happy. It means to shine the light of love onto the minds of as many wanderers as possible. It is also to help as many people as possible recover from the difficulties and setbacks of life, and to help them live their everyday lives in wisdom and courage.

Give with wisdom. Giving does not necessarily mean to provide materials or to give obsessively. True giving is the way to truly nurture people, and to do that, you must have wisdom.

So, let us walk a life of giving with wisdom and courage—a life of giving love to people unconditionally.

Love has no enemies. Love is invincible. For, true love is love that gives, or unconditional love; it is an infinite power that allows nothing to resist it. Love is a great river that flows from the infinite upstream to the infinite downstream. Moreover, no one can resist this great river. It is precisely because love is the power to give all and to push all downstream that no evil in this world can continue to resist love forever.

6

The Developmental Stages of Love

I have said many things about love up to this point. I have also mentioned about how true love is a love that gives, an unconditional love. The next true teaching of love that I must address is the developmental stages of love. Truly, love also has developmental stages. Even so, I'm sure not many people on earth have realized this.

The first stage is *fundamental love*. This stage can be said to be love in its simplest form. This would be the parental love for children and children's love for their parents; a man's love for a woman or a woman's love for a man; and the love for friends and neighbors. In its broadest form, fundamental love would include the love for the community and society as a whole.

Fundamental love is, of course, a form of giving love. It means the basis of this love comes from the feeling that you have for people you naturally care about. Having goodwill toward someone you naturally have concern toward is what fundamental love is. This is the most basic and common form of love, and is actually fairly difficult to practice.

This world on earth will surely become Heaven by simply filling it with fundamental love. Fundamental love is a form of love that everyone is expected to practice and it is possible for everyone to innately appreciate the beauty of it. This is because humans are by nature designed to feel happiness in giving love.

The question here is not only about how much you appreciate fundamental love, but also how you practice this love. If this fundamental love is practiced genuinely, this world on earth, while still being the third dimension, would turn into the fifth dimensional Goodness Realm of the Real World. Therefore, the prevalence of fundamental love is the first step to creating Heaven on Earth.

The second of the developmental stages of love is *nurturing love*. While fundamental love can be practiced by anyone, let alone the question of how you practice it, not everyone can practice nurturing love. That is because only capable people are able to nurture others. Unless you, with your own innate abilities and through effort, have firmly developed yourself to a degree where you can guide others, you will not be able to truly nurture others. What this means is, nurturing love is the love that can guide people. Therefore, before you can practice this love, you need to have first developed a distinguished character, for the blind cannot lead the blind.

Just as the water in a river flows from upstream to downstream, nurturing love also flows downward from the top. Nurturing love is an intellectual love, a rational love. You cannot truly guide others unless you have high intelligence to penetrate the true nature of people and society, and can take action to treat the main causes of existing problems by using a greater power of reasoning. At times, these practitioners of nurturing love must show "leader's anger" to those who are about to regress spiritually, and lead them in the right direction. Without doing so, people cannot truly be nurtured. In this sense, nurturing love can be said to be the love of the sixth dimensional Light Realm of the Real World. There are of course leaders on earth who are capable of practicing this love, and their minds are already attuned to the sixth dimension.

Fundamental love is the act of expressing goodwill toward someone you naturally care for, while nurturing love is the act of guiding others after having developed a distinguished character. Both are wonderful forms of love. However, nurturing love is still not enough. Anyone who has abilities or intelligence higher than that of others can practice it, but there is yet another stage of love that transcends ability, intellect, or putting in effort. Namely, it is the third stage of love: *forgiving love*.

The practitioners of forgiving love would have already taken a giant leap to attain a religious state of mind because this state can only be reached by those who have transcended good and evil and have devoted themselves to fulfill their individual mission. What this means is, people who attain this state have awakened and realized that those living in the third dimensional material world are spiritually blind, feeling their way with no sense of direction in the darkness. To have attained this, you need to have gone through a spiritual awakening in which you realized your own foolishness and repented. Only people who have found light through their own suffering can see the scales that are covering other people's eyes and love their Buddha-nature that lies within. This state of forgiving love can appear only after you have developed generosity and broad-mindedness, a virtue that surpasses abilities.

Only people who have truly understood and can see the true nature of human beings as children of Buddha or a part of God will be able to see the Buddha-nature that lies within, even of those who appear to be their enemies. This ability is called transcendental wisdom. In fact, this state of forgiving love is the state of bodhisattvas. The practitioners of this forgiving love are messengers from the seventh dimension, and their minds are attuned to the Bodhisattva Realm of the Real World.

This being said, however, forgiving love or the love of bodhisattva must never be mistakenly understood as a love that tolerates the workings of devils or aids them in their activities. Devils hinder and block the love that God gives to humans and their very existence is the antithesis of love. Bodhisattvas engage with devils using faith and egoless anger, or selfless wrath, as weapons. Indeed, some devils enter the gate of forgiveness only when they realize that they can never win against Buddha or God. For this reason, forgiving love would sometimes require a proactive approach.

In the next section, I will talk about yet a higher state of love.

7

Love Incarnate and Love of God

What is a higher love than forgiving love? I call it *love incarnate*. This form of love is no longer the love of one person for another; it even transcends status or position.

Love incarnate is embodied by a person whose very existence in this world, or whose momentary presence in your life, will help you overcome your problems and attain enlightenment, change your life completely, or guide you to correct your mistakes and enter the right path. The mere presence of such a person on earth will make the world of that age brighter and provide humankind with the light of hope. He or she loves, not because he or she loves a particular person, speaks beautiful words, or is kind; his or her very presence is love, and his or her character is love itself. We call such kind of people the manifestation of love incarnate. There certainly have been such brilliantly shining people throughout the history of humankind.

If we take forgiving love to be the love of highly virtuous religious leaders, then love incarnate would be the love of great figures that stand out in human history; they are the light of this world and the ethos of their age. Their love is not one-to-one; it is a one-to-many love that radiates in all directions. That is to say, they are light itself, or an embodiment of light.

You may understand what this level of love is—yes, this love belongs to the eighth dimensional Tathagata Realm. Someone achieving such greatness as to become love incarnate in a particular age is a tathagata, and the very fact that he or she is born on earth shows great mercy for humankind. Mercy is a light of love that illuminates the world far and wide. It is not a relative love that varies in strength depending on the person to whom it is being given. Mercy is, simply put, an absolute love and an impartial love.

Thus, fundamental love corresponds to the fifth dimension, nurturing love to the sixth, forgiving love to the seventh, and love incarnate to the eighth. These are the stages of love. It is good enough for you to know that these stages of love are your goals of love in spiritual training. Of course, there is the fourth dimensional love as well, which is instinctive love. Our minds can attune to Hell or to the Astral Realm (Fairy Realm) depending on how we deal with our instincts, but this is not the love to set as a goal in our spiritual discipline.

The highest form of love for humankind on planet Earth is that of the ninth dimension. This love is known as the embodiment of God or the love of a Savior. I do not suggest people to aim for this stage of love in their spiritual training because it is the love of those who have been chosen by God's (Buddha's) command as His instruments or supreme representatives. If misguided religious leaders attempt to preach the love of a Savior, what awaits them after death is not the world of the ninth dimension, but Abysmal Hell in the deepest pits of the fourth dimensional Hell Realm. The act of preaching the words of God (Buddha) incorrectly is a most terrible crime in the Real World, worse than robbery and murder, because it corrupts people's eternal souls, which are more precious than their lives on earth. Therefore, we must be content with simply knowing the fact that there is the love of God (or the great mercy of Buddha) above love incarnate, and that there has always been God's (Buddha's) great love to guide humanity, the love He sends for us to evolve.

To sum up, the developmental stages of love are as follows: the instinctive love of the fourth dimension, which does not require any effort; fundamental love, nurturing love, forgiving love and love incarnate, which can be a goal to which we aspire; and finally, the love of God that transcends the human mind.

8

Love and the Eightfold Path

In Chapter Two, I taught about the True Eightfold Path, and in the above passages I explained the developmental stages of love. Now, I would like to explain the relationship between these two teachings. Regarding the True Eightfold Path, I said that there are eight ways to live righteously as human beings. Further, they provide material to or the way to enlightenment that you should follow every day. In addition, I have taught you the developmental stages of love—fundamental love, nurturing love, forgiving love, and love incarnate—the four stages as levels of attainment for your spiritual training.

If we compare these two, the Eightfold Path is the method through which to practice your daily spiritual discipline; it focuses on your daily enlightenment. The developmental stages of love give you midterm levels and long-term goals to aim for as you practice them in your daily life. If we were to relate the Eightfold Path and the developmental stages of love as we seek for enlightenment, we can come to the following conclusion:

1. Right View and Right Speech
   lead to fundamental love;

2. Right Action and Right Living
   lead to nurturing love;

3. Right Thought and Right Effort
   lead to forgiving love;

4. Right Will and Right Meditation
   lead to love incarnate.

Let me explain the meaning of each of the previous statements. First, how do Right View and Right Speech lead to fundamental love? Fundamental love is the love for a person that you naturally care about. But to have the appropriate affection toward the person, you need to start by viewing him or her rightly, in the light of right faith. You need to be able to distinguish right from wrong. Without any biased ideas, you must see others rightly, exactly as they are, to know what they want now and what they are troubled with now. Once you are able to view rightly, next, speak rightly. That is to say, offer sound advice, not harmful words. Use heartwarming words or the right words that will help people in distress to recover.

Next, Right Action and Right Living lead to nurturing love. Right Action means to take the right course of action. During Shakyamuni's time, this meant to observe the precepts in order to prevent oneself from committing any physical sin. For example, followers were enjoined not to kill any living creatures including humans (no killing), not to steal anything (no stealing), and not to have sexual relations with anyone other than their spouse (no adultery). In modern terms, Right Action would mean to refrain from violence, stealing, and adultery, and to strive to improve one's moral standards as a member of society. It also means that one should act with adequate respect of other people's rights and character. As you refine your character as a member of society, you will be able to enlighten other people as well.

Right Living means to live your life in the correct manner, or to have a righteous lifestyle. It means to avoid any occupation or method of earning a living that would go against Buddha's Truth and would lead you to corruption, such as joining gangs, making a living in the illegal sex industry, or by performing any unnecessary slaughter. You must also avoid excessive alcohol consumption, gambling such as playing mahjong for money, excessive craving for horse racing or bicycle racing, as well as avoid drugs and smoking that would be detrimental to your health. A life of constantly being chased by loan sharks for having large debts is not considered Right Living, either. Also, humans cannot live alone; we receive support from many people and we help one another as we live in a community made up of all kinds of people. Thus, Right Living, or following a righteous life of faith in itself gives you the opportunity to help one another or to practice nurturing love. Right Living helps you guide one another. Put differently, the more people strive to create utopia in their homes and practice Right Living, the closer this world will be to Heaven. In these ways, practicing Right Action and Right Living mainly leads to practicing nurturing love.

Third, Right Thought and Right Effort lead to forgiving love. Firstly, Right Thought or thinking rightly means to view your relationships with other people through truthful eyes and try to make adjustments to improve those relationships without being swayed by the Three Poisons of the Mind (greed, anger, and ignorance) or the Six Worldly Delusions (conceit, doubt, and false views in addition to the Three Poisons of the Mind).[3] Instead of being deluded by how a person in front of you appears in this world, picture in your mind his or her true self as a being of the Real World and, based on that, consider the right kind of relationship you should have with that person. If you find any mistaken ideas in your mind, be remorseful and correct them. Then, as children of Buddha that you both are, contemplate how each of you should be. You should envision people trying to help one another as they aim to create great harmony. When you can think rightly, your mind will become very tolerant and you will develop a rich heart that can embrace everyone and everything. Thus, by refining yourself to this level, your mind will naturally progress to the state of forgiving love.

The same is true with Right Effort. To make the right effort in advancing on the path to the Truth means to focus your mind in earnest study to master Buddha's Truth. To deepen your state of enlightenment day by day, you must also make efforts to avoid temptations and fill your mind with good thoughts. When you make the right effort on the path to Buddha, your virtue will multiply and you will no longer have anger, complaints, dissatisfaction, or jealousy in your mind; literally, a life based on Right Thoughts will actually unfold, and there will be a world of great harmony on earth. That is to say, you will be able to maintain an unshakable mind all the time and have the power to rid wrongdoers of their sins. Therefore, the more you practice Right Effort, the deeper your religious insight will be, and that itself will enlarge your capacity of forgiving love.

Fourth, Right Will and Right Meditation lead to love incarnate. Right Will is to focus your mind on living in accordance with Buddha's Truth. It is to calm your mind and rightly plan your future as you pray to achieve self-realization in the appropriate way—these are the practices of Right Will. What does it mean for the seekers of Buddha's Truth to self-realize in the right way? This self-realization means to attain the perfect state of human as a child of Buddha. The state of being one with Buddha is the state of tathagata. It is the highest state for a human being. The very presence of such a person will earn him or her respect from people in the world; his or her very existence serves as a bright light for the people of the world. This is what Right Will aims for, and is the ultimate goal of a rightful life.

Right Meditation, or entering into a meditative state correctly, is the highest state for religious people and seekers of Buddha's Truth. Since ancient times, religious leaders have practiced different methods of concentrating their minds such as yoga, Zen, contemplation, and reflective meditation in efforts to communicate with high spirits. The first stage of Right Meditation begins from practicing daily self-reflection and communicating with your own guardian spirit. Next is having communication with guiding spirits, so that you can accomplish your holy mission. In the final stage, you would contact the guiding spirits of light in the upper realms or spirits in the Tathagata Realm.

The minds of living people can attune to three thousand worlds; when you attain the enlightenment of a tathagata, you can communicate with the great guiding spirits of the Tathagata Realm during Right Meditation. There is not a single tathagata of the eighth dimension born into a physical body who has not received direct or indirect guidance from the great guiding spirits of light in the upper realms. At the very least, they have received inspiration as they have performed their missions. There is no doubt about this.

The point is, the prerequisite to attain the stage of love incarnate is to have entered the meditative state rightly and become emancipated, thereby reaching the perfect state of right concentration.

What I have described so far, in other words, is that the Eightfold Path also has stages in its spiritual training. Self-reflection would be easier if you split it into four stages and practice them one by one, starting from Right View and Right Speech, followed by Right Action and Right Living, then Right Thought and Right Effort, and finally, Right Will and Right Meditation. This order is different from that which Shakyamuni Buddha had taught, but it is effective for beginners of the Truth.[4]

This can be said to be the same as practicing love in stages; once you have learned to practice fundamental love, you can next try to practice nurturing love; once you have passed that stage, you will be able to attempt the stage of forgiving love; then finally, you may attain the level of love incarnate. You cannot properly practice Right Action and Right Living, let alone Right

Thought and Right Effort, or Right Will and Right Meditation without the practice of Right View and Right Speech. Likewise, you cannot master nurturing love, forgiving love, and love incarnate without mastering fundamental love. In any case, the first stage is the most important to practice.

9

The Love of Angels

Now, let us turn our attention from humans, who are the objects of love and who try to practice it, to the ones who are the suppliers of love. I will move on to the topic of the love of angels in the higher Spirit World. In general, those referred to as angels are spirits who live in the upper part of the sixth dimensional Light Realm and higher. That is to say, they are various gods, bodhisattvas in the seventh dimension, tathagatas in the eighth dimension, and grand tathagatas in the ninth dimension, also known as great masters or great guiding spirits of light of the uppermost level.

Each of them has a different way of supplying love, or manifesting love, in the Real World. Arhats (angels of light) of the sixth dimension manifest their love in three ways. The first way is as guardian deities for the people on earth. The second way is as spirits who go to save those in Hell. The third way is as educators of spirits of the fifth dimensional Goodness Realm.

Bodhisattvas of light (angels) in the seventh dimension express their love in four ways. The first is that of leaders; they are born on earth to become leaders of a religion or of other fields and guide the people of the world. The second way is in service; they assist the work of the great guiding spirits of the Tathagata Realm. The third way is to be in charge of saving the spirits in Hell. The fourth way is to be suppliers of light in the

Real World; Buddha's light is supplied to the worlds of the sixth dimension and lower through bodhisattvas.

Tathagatas (archangels) in the eighth dimension express their love in five ways. The first is to preach new religious teachings in this world; they are born every several hundred years to start a new religion or to become a great religious reformer. The second is to be instructors of bodhisattvas; each tathagata guides dozens of bodhisattvas and every bodhisattva has a tathagata for his or her teacher. The third is as commanders of legions that oppose satanic spirits in Hell and try to convert them. The fourth is to specialize in and spread one of the prismatic colors of Buddha's light—for example, the light of love. The fifth is the creative love to execute plans for a new civilization.

The love of grand tathagatas of light or great guiding spirits of light in the ninth dimension encompasses all forms of love, but their love can be classified into six major types. The first is the love as a savior who is born into this world every few thousand years to found a global religion and to purify the world. The second is the love of instructors who give guidance, from the Real World, to the saviors born on earth. The third is the love which propels the evolution of humankind. The fourth is as a source of one of the seven colors of Buddha's light; this love is supplied as a specific light to the worlds of the eighth dimension and lower. The fifth is the love of regulators who maintain order in the Real World; they serve as role models or yardsticks to gauge how much souls have progressed in their states of mind. Finally, the sixth is the love of those ultimately responsible for plans regarding Earth, as a part of the vaster plans of the universe.

10

The Great River of Love

So far, I have discussed many aspects of the love of humans and of angels. These show that love flows not only through this world of the third dimension, but also through the multidimensional world of the fourth dimension and higher. What is the essence of love? It is life that runs like a powerful river; it is like the continual surge of water that flows rapidly. Actually, looking at the worlds from the ninth to the third dimensions using spiritual sight, I can see a great river of love, with its source in the dimensions infinitely far above, flowing from the ninth dimension to the eighth, seventh, sixth, fifth, fourth, and to the third as a tremendous flow of energy. This is truly a spectacular sight and a wonderful panorama.

Love, in other words, is a great river. It is a power that flows from the upper reaches downstream without ever stopping; it is life with a momentum that nothing can resist. Love has no enemies. Once you actually see this spiritual panorama of the great river of love, you will clearly know that nothing can stand against love.

Do you imagine Hell to be powerful enough to rival Heaven, that is, the world of God (Buddha)? Do you think Hell is an enormous world that is just as large as Heaven? If you do, you are mistaken. The great river named love, originating from God (Buddha), flows from the upstream regions far above, washing away everything with its extremely strong current. The fourth dimension, of which Hell is a part, is located further downstream near the mouth of the river. No matter how hard seawater, which contains the salty impurities of material arrogance, desires, delusion, and evil, tries to turn the river water into salt water, the seawater cannot do so. It cannot stand against the unstoppable power of the great river of love that rushes forth.

Love is light. Just as no darkness can conquer light, no evil can conquer love and no Hell can block the river of love forever. Hell is not a force powerful enough to resist Heaven. Hell is like cancer cells in a part of the world God (Buddha) created, mere salt water trying to seep into the fresh water of a river.

Since ancient times, people have been imagining Hell to be a world equal in size to Heaven; they have been thinking that angels and devils are evenly matched. But this is not true. Heaven, or more precisely the heavenly world, stretches from the Astral Realm of the fourth dimension to the dimensions far up, whereas Hell is only the muddy portion within the fourth dimension, a shaded area where the light does not reach.

It is certainly true that this murky portion has grown large enough to sustain a population of several billion. But just as any ice will melt under the light of the sun, Hell is destined to disappear. The influence of Hell is overestimated only because the spiritual field that Hell occupies is located very close to the earthly world and the spiritual vibrations of both worlds easily affect one another.

Then, what are the elements that make up Hell? Here are the thought energies or elements whirling around in Hell:

envy, jealousy, anger that comes from feelings and instinct, complaints, feelings of discontent, dissatisfaction, pessimistic thoughts, negative thoughts, indecisiveness, cowardice, laziness, self-hatred, grudges, hatred, cursing, lust, self-assertion, egotism, abusive speech, double-dealing, manic depression, uncontrollable drinking, violence, exclusionism, lies, falsehood, materialism, atheism, loneliness, authoritarianism, greed for money, status, and fame, and disharmony. These are all negative energies. However, these are not substantial energies at all. The bottom line is, hatred, jealousy, anger, and dissatisfaction, for instance, are all caused by the absence of love. They simply lack the energy of love.

In short, the spirits in Hell are not at all powerful beings who can withstand the light of the heavenly world; they, too, are beings who want to be loved. In truth, evil spirits want to be loved even more than they are now. They want to be treated kindly by many people. Deep inside, they crave more and more love. Therefore, in actuality, they are unfortunate, pitiful beings who must be saved. They are unfortunate patients who suffer from a "love deficiency syndrome."

Earlier, I said that to love is to give first. But Hell is full of spirits always craving something; they want others to do something for them. In the end, those who did not understand the essence of love and lived a life of taking love are now suffering in Hell.

It is still not too late to dissolve Hell. We can do this by having all people *awaken to the essence of love—to give*. This being so, what will you give first? Giving love starts from showing gratitude. First, be grateful for the fact that you have been given everything from Buddha. Then, you will naturally want to give something back to the world He created as a way to repay Him. This is the first step to start giving love to others.

ENDNOTES

1 Here, the word "God" refers to the image of God Hermes. Hereafter in this chapter, the term "God" used in the Christian sense will refer to Lord El Cantare.

2 The statement, "God is love," shows the awareness (enlightenment) Jesus possessed—the true nature of Lord El Cantare is the God of Love.

3 The Three Poisons of the Mind—greed, anger, and ignorance—are negative mental functions, or worldly desires, that defile one's Buddha-nature. These combined with conceit, doubt, and various false views make up the Six Worldly Delusions. Right Thought as taught in traditional Buddhism states that the Six Worldly Delusions are the major causes that delude people's right thinking and lead them to Hell. But as the expression "human beings have 108 worldly desires" suggests, there are numerous negative mental functions, and therefore, there is no limit to how deeply we must practice Right Thought.

4 Happy Science members, who are regarded as professionals engaging in spiritual training, are recommended to practice "Words of Emancipation: Buddha's Teaching, The Eightfold Path," the fifth sutra in our basic sutra book, *Buddha's Teaching: The Dharma of the Right Mind*.

CHAPTER FOUR

THE
ULTIMATE
OF
ENLIGHTENMENT

1

What Is Enlightenment?

Enlightenment is what human beings have always sought throughout the ages. Even if we do not know exactly what enlightenment is, we find that we have the desire to develop and improve ourselves further in our search for enlightenment. This cannot be denied. While enlightenment is particularly associated with religion, there is a fundamental and strong impulse to attain enlightenment in philosophy as well. The philosophical desire for enlightenment is the desire to attain the Truth, the yearning to understand the mysteries and workings of the world in an intellectual and rational way. Whether or not Confucianism is a religion is open to discussion, but there is no doubt that Confucius taught the way to human perfection and the ultimate state of moral perfection. In other words, Confucius tried to guide humans to attain enlightenment from an educational standpoint by teaching them the Way.

In this chapter, I would like to mainly focus on religious enlightenment, which includes the philosophical desire to find the Truth and the way to human perfection in a moral sense. The vital point in religious enlightenment is that it is discussed in connection with Buddha. In truth, enlightenment means to become closer to Buddha as we explore and discover the principles of the world that He created. In this respect, there is no limit to enlightenment. To put it another way, you can never say you have "fully attained enlightenment" because no matter how much effort you put forth, it's almost impossible to gain a complete understanding of the entire Real World. You would need almost eternal effort to come even close to Buddha. This being said, however, there are different levels of enlightenment, so you could say that you have attained enlightenment of a certain level. There is also the highest level of enlightenment that human beings with physical bodies on earth can attain. Thus, I would like to elaborate on the different stages leading to this highest level of enlightenment for human beings.

Of all the great religious leaders and masters in the past that people today have kept record of, the one who pursued enlightenment most thoroughly was Shakyamuni Buddha (Gautama Siddhartha), who preached the Laws more than 2,500 years ago in India. From the time he attained enlightenment under a bodhi tree and became Buddha, his level of enlightenment continued to rise until he passed away at age eighty under sal trees on the outskirts of Kushinagar. This is written in various records, but most of them capture only fragments of his philosophy and fail to convey the actual state of enlightenment he attained.

The world of the mind is full of wonders. It has been more than a decade since I opened the door of my mind and learned how to communicate with the spirits in my subconscious mind. During this time, I came to have a clear understanding of what the saints of the past actually felt and did, as well as the thoughts they had and the enlightenment they attained. The world of the mind is truly mysterious. I can easily see the content of

Shakyamuni Buddha's enlightenment that he attained under a bodhi tree. Although it happened more than 2,500 years ago, I can feel it as if it were happening this very moment.

Primarily, this chapter focuses on the enlightenment of Shakyamuni Buddha, as I try to offer an opportunity to reconsider enlightenment in the world of today. I want to pass on the wisdom regarding enlightenment to future generations because the methodology to attain enlightenment is the legacy of past humankind and the hope for future humankind.

2

The Merit of Enlightenment

For what reasons exactly do human beings strive for enlightenment? Suppose you attained enlightenment, what would you be able to gain from it? Before dealing with these questions, we first need to consider the true purpose and mission of human beings. Why are humans born on earth? Why are we born with physical bodies? These are the starting points.

Before you were born as a human, you were living freely in the heavenly world as a spirit. In the heavenly world, you do not need to eat to stay alive. You do not need to earn money to support yourself. You do not need to endure the nine months in your mother's womb, or always cry because you cannot understand things as an infant. You have no frustration over sexual issues in adolescence or conflicts between parent and child. You have no financial worries or distress of being used by people at work. You have no pain of meeting someone you don't like, or sorrow from parting with someone you love. You have no suffering of aging, being ill, losing your looks, or being abandoned by your children or grandchildren. You have no pain of parting with your spouse through death or the fear of your own death that you will eventually have to face. There is absolutely no such suffering in the heavenly world.

In the heavenly world, our minds can be seen as clearly as through a glass window. Therefore, those with inharmonious thoughts cannot remain with others. Thus, you only meet wonderful people who understand each other, every day. Everyone there loves and nurtures each other. The spirits there can also freely change their age and appearance as they like. When they need something, they only need to focus their will strongly to manifest it before their eyes. Everyone is earnestly undergoing spiritual discipline at his or her level, aiming to attain a higher awakening of the Truth.

Disharmonious spirits in Hell can never be born into the earthly world as human beings. Their minds are full of combative and destructive thoughts, and spirits with such minds are not allowed to inhabit human bodies. What do spirits need to do to be reborn on earth? Firstly, they must be living in the fourth dimensional Astral Realm (Fairy Realm), or higher. They need to awaken even slightly, as heavenly beings, that they are spiritual beings and children of Buddha. Otherwise, they cannot be reborn into this world. Those who haven't at least completed the required level of self-reflection are not allowed to reincarnate. In this sense, being reborn on earth is, from the outset, a kind of trial for those in the heavenly world. And for those who have spent many years in Hell and have finally finished their self-reflection, it is a chance to start over as human beings and try again.

For this reason, this world is a training ground. For the spirits who were living freely in the heavenly world, being born into a physical body means actually being tested as to their spirituality and their Buddha-nature. This world is a place where one's spiritual awakening is being thoroughly tested to see if it is truly genuine. It is easy to believe in Buddha when you are spiritually free. But as you lead a life bound by the rules of this third dimensional material world, how much can you understand the rules of the fourth dimension and higher, the power of Buddha, and that the power is at work in this world? You are thoroughly tested on these points, and only when you pass these tests can you return to a higher world than the one you came from.

Those who have long suffered in Hell but have finally reached the state to self-reflect and attained the lowest level of enlightenment for humans as children of Buddha have a strong determination to be praiseworthy persons when they are born again on earth. However, being severely affected by the coarse vibrations of the third dimensional material world, some will deeply indulge themselves in worldly desires without awakening to their true nature as children of Buddha, and end up descending to an even darker part of Hell without returning to the heavenly world.

This third dimensional material world, or the phenomenal world, is indeed such a severe training ground for the soul. At the same time, though, there is hope. All kinds of people, including those you would never be able to encounter in the Real World, can meet each other in this third dimensional world. You have a chance to meet different kinds of people, including perhaps a great guiding spirit of light in the flesh as well as someone whose mind is attuned to devils of Hell. Everyone begins on the same starting line when they are newborns; they are given a chance to start their lives afresh equally. Thus, the merit of enlightenment is that we can redo our lives.

3

Ways of Enlightenment

How, then, can human beings attain enlightenment? This is the next question. Enlightenment is for humans to further refine their spirituality and Buddha-nature as they redo their lives, and when we think about how to do this, we will notice that we have already been provided with various opportunities and infinite ways. Various opportunities, in other words, mean the various ways of spiritual training. Not only Buddhism, but also Christianity, Shintoism, Confucianism, Taoism and Islam all have some form of spiritual discipline. This is the very reason why people living on earth end up in the woods or a maze as they seek the way to Buddha. In the end, rather than wondering which way of spiritual training they should choose, they get caught up wondering which religion is true and correct.

All major world religions are, in some way, manifestations of Buddha's light. Leaving aside new local religions, religions that have never ceased to touch people's hearts for hundreds or thousands of years have leaders who continue to earn respect from people. The lives of such religious leaders have some form of brilliance that embodies Buddha's light. However, their brilliance shines with a somewhat different hue depending on the circumstances of the time, ethnicity and culture of the region in which the teachings were given. Nevertheless, the teachings of the past are merely teachings of the past, and the coming new age will require new teachings. What is urgently needed is the appearance of new teachings. There is a need to search for new ways of spiritual training.

Ways to attain enlightenment are, ultimately, means to make your state of mind one with Buddha's mind. They are the ways to live with Buddha's mind as your own; they explore how you can live in accordance with the Truth. One way to do this is to practice the True Eightfold Path, and another is to practice the developmental stages of love. If you wish to take a Buddhist approach, I recommend that you live with the True Eightfold Path as your daily guideline because it teaches the universal Buddha's Truth. It is the way to human perfection, which you cannot completely master, no matter how much you try.

How many people are able to view right, think right, and speak right? How many people can act right and live right? And how many people have mastered making right effort, holding right will, and entering right meditation, which are the deep principles of Buddha's Laws? In short, the way of the Eightfold Path is one specific method to attain enlightenment that you cannot master even in a lifetime.

Just practicing the introductory level of Right View and Right Speech of the Eightfold Path properly will certainly take at least five to ten years. Once you feel confident practicing them, next, try concentrating on practicing Right Action and Right Living every day. If you can practice these four paths correctly, you should be able to attain the enlightenment of the sixth dimensional Light Realm.

The practice of Right Thought and Right Effort will put you at the starting line of an advanced religious life. If you manage to build a mind that is as durable as steel, that enables you to live through any hardships you may face in life with an unshakable mind, you have achieved the state of arhat. The arhat state is a gateway to pass from the sixth dimensional Light Realm to the seventh dimensional Bodhisattva Realm; it is a state in which you have virtually finished developing yourself. Those who become anxious from slight remarks that people make, fly into a rage over trifling matters, or are driven by the desire for social status or fame have yet to reach the state of arhat.

There are many contemporary religious leaders in Japan and around the world, but first, take a good look at their minds and deeds. Some concentrate only on gaining psychic powers, while others take advantage of the weaknesses of others to deceive them. Some even extort money from their followers by glaring at them and threatening that they will fall to Hell or receive divine punishment. Such people are a long way from reaching the state of arhat, the first step to becoming a bodhisattva of light. As long as one's mind is swayed by the desire for social status, fame, money, or by lust, anger, hatred or complaints, he or she can never be called a divine religious leader.

The basic way to enlightenment is to first aim to reach the state of arhat, where your mind is undisturbed by worldly matters, is always pure and clear, is attuned to your guardian spirit, and it is where you can very clearly understand the feelings of others.

Unless you pass through this gateway, you cannot go further with your spiritual training or enlightenment. So, you should first aim to attain the state of arhat. In the enlightenment beyond this level lies the world of those who have awakened to the real Truth.

4

Nyoshin

Deep enlightenment. What is the state of mind that is even deeper than the state of arhat? The arhat state is a stage where you have established firm faith in Buddha and developed an unshakable mind that does not waver in the face of worldly troubles. You will be receiving guidance from your guardian spirit as you live each day and know the feelings of the people you pass by as if you are seeing into their minds. In other words, at this stage you are very close to becoming complete as a human and have reached a level where you can teach and guide common people from a religious standpoint.

Nonetheless, even at this stage, you are still at risk of falling because the arhat state is merely a state in which you have gone through self-reflection deep enough to be able to communicate with your guardian spirit in your subconscious mind; you have yet to deeply understand the minds of bodhisattvas of light. You haven't yet thoroughly grasped the levels, varieties, and profoundness of the teachings of Buddha's Truth, so there is still high risk you may be deluded by heresies and false teachings.

When inhabitants of the Tengu (goblins) and Sennin (hermit sorcerers) Realms in Rear Heaven attain this state, they may exert a rudimentary level of divine supernatural power to psychically read things or cause spiritual phenomena. What you must do is to make efforts to deepen your state of love and enlightenment. Never think little of the study of the Truth.

There is another reason why people fall from the state of arhat. Figuratively speaking, the arhat state of mind is like metal that begins to shine after rust is removed from its surface. But since it has yet to be rustproofed, if you forget to polish it for some time, rust will soon develop again. For this reason, if you do not notice your mind getting rusty, but rather believe and act like you are a great teacher who has attained enlightenment, then you are in great danger.

When your mind is shining brightly, its surface is very smooth, so even if any negative thoughts come at you, it has the power to repel them. But when your mind gets rusty, its surface becomes rough, so it traps many negative thoughts or things. Then, there will be beings that drive pitons into this rough surface and hang ropes to climb up—the devils of Hell. Various creatures from the world of total darkness will climb up the ropes that hang right to the bottom of Hell. These include suffering spirits, animal spirits and even devils. In this way, some religious leaders, in spite of having managed to reach the state of arhat, unfortunately allow evil to sneak into their minds. And they delude the public and lead them astray. This is the most dangerous pitfall.

Therefore, it is crucial that you remove the rust from your mind to keep it rust-free, every day. Polish it well until it's sparkling clean. This is crucial. For, if your mind is left rusty and rough, you never know when a devil could drive a piton into it with a rope attached. You may try hard to knock the devil off, but you will have another piton driven in from behind. When this happens, there is little you can do. A simple act of spiritual purification or exorcism will not truly save you because no matter how many times you exorcise the devils, they will keep creeping back in unless you remove the rust from your mind. You need to make it shine. This is why polishing your mind is crucial. If possible, add coating or do some rustproofing because making it rustproof will enable you to attain higher enlightenment.

The state of enlightenment above arhat is called *nyoshin*. Nyoshin is a stage where you are able to receive guidance from the higher levels of the Spirit World, from those whose spiritual level is higher than that of your guardian spirit. In other words, at this stage you can communicate spiritually with guiding spirits, meaning the high spirits residing in the seventh dimensional Bodhisattva Realm and higher. When you reach this state, you are virtually indomitable. Except under extreme conditions, you will no longer fall into the hands of those in the world of devils because once you start receiving guidance from tathagatas and bodhisattvas, you will emit a stronger light that keeps evil away.

When you attain the state of nyoshin, you are always humble and show no arrogance. Your everyday concerns are mainly about how to be of service to others; in other words, how to contribute to the world or save those who are lost. Most of the time, conceit is the cause of people's fall from the state of arhat, but once you achieve the indomitable state of nyoshin, egoism or self-centeredness will disappear, so your mind is always serene. It is at this stage that you can practice Right Will and Right Meditation in the truest sense.

The state of nyoshin has another attribute. In fact, as you approach the state of *avalokitesvara*, you will be able to readily know the condition of people who are hundreds of miles away. For example, just by looking at someone's name, even if the person is on the opposite side of the globe, you can instantly grasp that person's current state of mind, suffering, and the spirits possessing him or her, as well as the person's past life, the life before that and more, and even the future lives. Even so, you must keep deepening your love and elevating your wisdom in order to prevent yourself from solely developing the ability of clairvoyance as sennins of Rear Heaven do.

5

Avalokitesvara

Nyoshin is the state of mind of bodhisattvas, who are experts in the esoteric principles of the Spirit World. It even leads to the Tathagata Realm. There are different levels of nyoshin, but generally, the level of nyoshin above arhat implies the state of mind of the bodhisattva. This not only means those people who have attained enlightenment in the earthly world, but also those who share a similar state in the other world, or the Real World.

However, just being spirits in the other world does not mean that they are all-knowing. Of course, the scope of what they can understand or grasp varies depending on their level of awareness and enlightenment. A typical example of this is foresight. Any spirit of the fourth dimension or higher in the Real World can foresee things that have yet to happen or future events, although the extent of this ability varies on the spirit. But when people of the third dimensional world on earth are involved, there can often be a problem because things sometimes turn out different in terms of time or place.

To explain further, there are two reasons. The first is that there are fixed events and fluid events in regards to future events. Fixed events are what have already been decided in the higher realms of the Spirit World and cannot be changed except under extremely rare conditions. Fluid events, on the other hand, are merely what are likely to happen if things keep going the way they are going now. So, these events can be changed by the efforts of people on earth and of their guardian and guiding spirits. Thus, the spirits in the heavenly world sometimes cannot predict accurately.

The second reason is that, depending on the levels of consciousness and areas of strengths and weaknesses of the heavenly spirits, their predictions will vary in precision. Generally speaking, it is true that the higher one's spiritual level, the more accurate one's foresight is. Some spirits even specialize in foresight as their profession, and there is a higher chance that the predictions of such experts are correct.

Now I would like to describe avalokitesvara, a state of enlightenment higher than that of nyoshin. The Heart Sutra starts with the phrase, "Aryavalokitesvaro bodhisattvo gambhiram prajnaparamita caryam caramano vyavalokayati," which translates as, "when Avalokitesvara Bodhisattva has deepened his state of spiritual training and has accessed the treasure of the inner subconscious." Avalokitesvara Bodhisattva is not the name of a person. It is the state of a bodhisattva who has attained the avalokitesvara level, a level with the ability to see through everything, by advancing in spiritual training.

Bodhisattva is the level of souls that have roughly completed the Hinayana stage of building themselves and have entered the Mahayana stage, that is to say, souls that have stood up for salvation, wanting to save all people. Even at this state of bodhisattva, however, you still have personal worries and suffering, so your condition to exert divine supernatural power

(Dharma power) is not constant. But as you further refine your state and advance to attain the state of brahma, the highest level of enlightenment in the Bodhisattva Realm, you will become able to exert divine powers consistently regardless of mild illness, minor mishaps, and trivial human relationship problems. Put simply, Avalokitesvara Bodhisattva is the state of brahma, and in the Real World it refers to souls that have reached the realm between the Bodhisattva Realm and the Tathagata Realm, the spiritual zone that can be called either the seventh dimension or eighth dimension.

At this stage, although perhaps not sufficiently, spirits have acquired all six divine supernatural powers. The six divine supernatural powers are *tengen* (spiritual sight), *ten'ni* (spiritual hearing), *tashin* (mind reading), *shukumyo* (fate reading), *jinsoku* (astral travel), and *rojin* (extinction of worldly desires). Let me explain each power.

Tengen is the ability to see spiritual things; it is the power to see auras of living people or the spirits possessing them, or even to see through to the other world, or the Real World. Ten'ni is the ability to hear voices of spirits of the other world. The ability to channel spiritual messages is one form of this power. Tashin is the ability to read other people's minds and to readily understand their feelings. Shukumyo is the ability to not only see your own future, but also the ability to read people's Thought Tape to readily understand their fate and destiny. Of course, you will come to know their past lives as well. Jinsoku is also known as out-of-body experience; with this ability, you can see and hear the Spirit World, all while leaving your physical body on earth, and you can use teleportation. Rojin is the state described when Confucius declared, "I followed my heart's desire without overstepping the line" (*The Analects*). It is the power to transcend all worldly desires at will without their controlling you. This power is also the ability to make efforts and discipline yourself to keep removing the rust from your mind very thoroughly, even after you have acquired spiritual powers.[1]

Avalokitesvara Bodhisattvas are those who have begun to develop the abovementioned six divine supernatural powers in some way. This is clearly a higher state than nyoshin, where you can read the minds of a multitude of people simultaneously or readily understand the mind of someone who is far away.

6

One Is Many—Many Are One

Now I would like to talk about the enlightenment attained after your spiritual training as a human reaches the deepest level of Right Thought, Right Effort, Right Will, and Right Meditation, or the stage of love incarnate in the developmental stages of love. To put it differently, in this section, I will delve right into the enlightenment of the Tathagata Realm.

Up until the state of bodhisattva, your recognition of the soul is still somewhat bound by human forms or appearances. Spirits are essentially energy body without shape, or intelligence without appearance. However, after being born countless times as human beings in the long years of reincarnation, many spirits become used to being restrained by their image as human-like souls and are unable to function freely as they originally could. In short, in the seventh dimensional Bodhisattva Realm, the spirits are still undergoing spiritual training in human form. Humans have two arms and two legs, wear clothes, have a hairstyle, and have facial features. This is the only way that most bodhisattvas can recognize themselves. They feel uncomfortable unless they have a human appearance, even in the other world. So, although they are highly virtuous and possess very strong leadership skills, their spiritual power is limited due to their humanness.

However, things are different in the eighth dimensional Tathagata Realm. Spirits of this realm know that they are not souls in human form. For them, souls in human forms are simply memories of their residing in human bodies in the long years of reincarnation. Tathagatas know that spirits are intellectual energy, or shapeless bodies of light; they not only understand this from a knowledge basis, but they know it from actual experience in their lives.

Suppose a psychic living on earth could send his or her soul to the eighth dimensional Tathagata Realm while leaving his or her physical body here on earth. What would the soul see? To a person from earth, the spirits in the eighth dimensional Tathagata Realm would appear in human form as in their previous life on earth, so they would look familiar to the person. They would then invite the guest from earth into their homes and would offer him or her coffee or wine, which would be quite delicious with a fragrance that cannot be found anywhere on earth. Then, the psychic would report the occurrence as follows: "The eighth dimensional Tathagata Realm is truly an amazing world. The spirits there are like gods, the streets are paved with rubies, and the buildings are adorned with diamonds in many places. Their drinks have flavors that are so rich, they cannot be found on earth. The table was made of shining marble and there were four magnificent crystal pillars in the corners of the room."

Emanuel Swedenborg, a famous psychic in modern Europe, reported his visit to the Spirit World in a similar way. But this kind of scene is due to the lack of spiritual awareness of people like him; if we look harder and examine the scene, the jewel-encrusted buildings and streets will disappear and the tathagata will simply be standing there alone smiling. If we look even harder through our spiritual eyes, the tathagata will also disappear and there will only be a giant mass of light. In other words, tathagatas are just making their world understandable using rubies, diamonds, and other jewels to show hospitality to a person from an earthly dimension.

In this way, the enlightenment of tathagatas has reached a stage where they can recognize themselves as formless entities. So, if there is anyone living on earth who has attained the enlightenment of tathagata, he or she should be well aware of the law of the Tathagata Realm: one is many—many are one. Put differently, in the world of tathagatas, you cannot recognize "one" as something objective. So, what you recognize as "one" can be "ten" or "ten thousand," while what you recognize as "one thousand" can be "one." Consciousness, which is absolute existence, does not appear as a set number. It can appear in as many a number of ways it will work. Only the unifying consciousness knows its true state.

Let me make this easier to understand. If one tathagata has ten tasks, it will manifest itself into ten people and if it has ten thousand tasks, it will appear as ten thousand people. But even if it splits into ten thousand people, there is a unifying consciousness that recognizes those people as one.

Kitaro Nishida (1870 - 1945), founder of the Kyoto school of philosophy in Japan, seems to have been aware of this law of the Tathagata Realm as a result of his philosophical study. He was originally from the Tathagata Realm, which is naturally why the beings in his own subconscious were telling him that such a world exists. This eighth dimension is a world where "absolutely contradictory self-identity" is a reality. The realm where what may appear to the eyes as diverse, and even contradictory, can be intuitively unified as one. This is the Tathagata Realm. Apparently, the philosopher Kitaro Nishida partially experienced the enlightenment of the Tathagata Realm while he was still alive on earth.

7

The Enlightenment of the Sun Realm

The enlightenment of the Tathagata Realm is the enlightenment of "one is many—many are one," that surpasses the bodily senses of humans. It is a state where you fully awaken to the truth that spirits are particles of Buddha's light, energy form without shape, and intelligence without appearance. This state is almost the highest state that human beings living on earth can attain. The Earth Spirit Group has tens of billions of spirits, but there are only a few, less than 500 spirits, in the eighth dimensional Tathagata Realm. This shows how hard it is to attain the enlightenment of tathagata. The enlightenment of tathagata transcends the duality of good and evil, to the stage of unification or sublation. So, refining yourself through life training alone is not enough; you need to have the clear reasoning ability and the penetrating power of enlightenment to understand and master the magnificent drama and laws of the universe.

Who are the spirits in the eighth dimensional Tathagata Realm who were born in Japan? Apart from those in the age of gods, they include Shotoku Taishi (Prince Shotoku; 574 - 622) from just before the Taika Reforms in the mid-seventh century, the Buddhist monk Kukai (774 - 835) of the Heian period, and the aforementioned philosopher Kitaro Nishida of the Showa period. There are a few more besides them.

There are fewer than 500 tathagatas in the eighth dimensional Tathagata Realm, which is roughly divided into four levels. The lowest level is the upper part of the Brahma Realm, where about 40 tathagatas reside. Next is the Semi-Divine Realm, with about 120 tathagatas. Above that is the Light Divine Realm, with about 280 tathagatas. And the highest level of the eighth dimension is the Sun Realm, in the strict sense. In a broader sense, the Sun Realm includes the Cosmic Realm of the ninth dimension, but in the strict sense of the Sun Realm, there are about 20 grand tathagatas who are halfway between the eighth and ninth dimensions.

Who are the grand tathagatas in this Sun Realm? In the Shinto line, there is Kamu-Musuhi-no-Kami. In the Christian line, there are Augustine and Thomas Aquinas. Lao-tzu of Taoism and Mo-tzu of Mohism are in this Sun Realm as well, as are the Greek philosophers Socrates and Plato. In the Buddhist line, there are Akshobhya Tathagata and Bhaisajyaguru Tathagata, along with others. Muhammad of Islam seems to be in the Divine Light Realm, which is one realm below the Sun Realm.

So, what is the enlightenment of the Sun Realm that all these spirits have in common? In short, it is no longer the enlightenment of a human. It is not a state that can be attained by personal efforts; inhabitants of the Sun Realm are given the status of a god. You cannot reach the levels of enlightenment of the Sun Realm and above through spiritual training as a human. These spirits belong to the esteemed ranks of the grand spirits, and are revered as the Primordial God in most religions.

On what grounds am I saying that their level of enlightenment is beyond the enlightenment of humans? The spirits in the Sun Realm are directly involved in planning the evolution of humanity on Earth. It is mainly these spirits of the Sun Realm who help the grand spirits of the ninth dimensional Cosmic Realm. They are the ones planning, designing, and carrying out in a tangible way, the blossoming of civilizations on Earth, innovation of religion and the rise of new eras, etc.

8

The Enlightenment of Shakyamuni Buddha (1): The Great Enlightenment

Before I move on to the enlightenment of the ninth dimensional Cosmic Realm, let me first talk about the enlightenment that Gautama Siddhartha, or Shakyamuni Buddha, attained in India more than two thousand years ago. At the age of twenty-nine, Gautama Siddhartha renounced the world. Then, at the age of thirty-five, after six years of austere and ascetic training, he left this practice and attained enlightenment under a bodhi tree. After about a week of meditation, he entered into a deep state of meditation from around one o'clock at night. In this state, he awakened to the following Truth.

"For many years, I barely ate or drank. I have practiced asceticism, believing that I could take a great leap spiritually and attain enlightenment by mortifying my physical body to its absolute limit. Six years have already passed since I fled from Kapilavastu, leaving my wife, Yashodhara, and my son, Rahula, and walking out on my father, King Suddhodana, who wanted me to succeed him to the throne. When I lived in Kapilavastu, I was strong and muscular, adept at both military and literary arts. But look at me now. My ribs stand out, I have sunken eyes, and I am just skin and bone. If tormenting our bodies is the purpose of soul training in life, then what would be the point of having life in physical bodies at all? If the Primordial Buddha[2] wanted human beings to deny the flesh, wouldn't that imply that those who commit suicide are the most awakened?

"But what can we achieve through suicide? All rules in the great universe exist through the chain of cause and effect; if we sow a bad seed, we will surely have to reap a bad fruit. If we create another cause of suffering by committing suicide, what awaits us would no doubt be bitter anguish in Hell in the other world. The practice of austere and ascetic training that tortures the physical body is none other than an act of gradual suicide. The state of Buddha is a state of tranquility, but there is no tranquility in ascetic training. The cause of enlightenment cannot be found in ascetic training. What I have gained as a result of my six years of training are a horrible appearance that shocks people and harsh eyes that pierce sharply. Through ascetic training I only acquired a strict attitude; my harsh, piercing eyes show absolutely no love or mercy. How can I be truly kind and compassionate toward others when I cannot find peace of mind in myself and have no sense of happiness in myself?

"But what exactly is this sense of happiness within me? When I lived as a prince in Kapilavastu, everyone cherished me and I had all the money, women, and luxuries that I could ask for. But was there a sense of happiness in my heart? I was actually filled with dullness as I lived in the arms of comfort; there were always hunger and thirst in my heart. My mind was constantly wavering with inner conflicts, entangled with all kinds of desires and intentions of other people. I was destined to be king one day, so I would have had to lead my people, go to war against neighboring lands, and cause terrible bloodshed as a result.

"To seek worldly status and fame only leads to emptiness. My life in Kapilavastu was not at all a life of true happiness. I felt spiritually unfulfilled, and I lived in increasing anxiety and frustration. Happiness for human beings is found not in stagnation and laziness. Happiness for human beings is found in daily spiritual progress. We find true happiness not in worldly success. True happiness for a human, born as a child of the Primordial Buddha, is found in the improvement of our spirituality and Buddha-nature according to the Will of the Primordial Buddha.

"True enlightenment and true happiness for humans, the children of the Primordial Buddha, are found neither in the extravagant life of royalty nor in extremely austere and ascetic training. We cannot find true enlightenment, true happiness, or true peace of mind in a life of pleasing our bodies in an extreme way or a life of hurting our bodies in an extreme way. The true way of living for human beings is to abandon both extremes and to seek the Truth in the Middle Way. Only when we live a balanced life can we find the Middle Way, and in the Middle Way there is brought forth a world of great harmony where we are not bound by pain or pleasure.

"The life that humans are truly aspiring to live is a life of great harmony. When all people abandon the extremes of pain and pleasure, enter the Middle way, and practice the Eightfold Path of Right View, Right Thought, Right Speech, Right Action, Right Living, Right Effort, Right Will, and Right Meditation, we can create a true kingdom of the mind, as well as a true Buddhaland.

"So, true happiness for humans is to be found in our spiritual joy and making spiritual progress in our daily lives. Our sense of happiness will increase in the course of practicing and mastering the depths of the Eightfold Path."

9

The Enlightenment of Shakyamuni Buddha (2): Entering Nirvana

In the previous section, I wrote about Shakyamuni's state of mind when he attained great enlightenment at the age of thirty-five. The content of his great awakening that took place 2,500 years ago unfolds before my eyes as my pen writes the words. I believe it would easily take up an entire book if I were to describe all his enlightenment. But for now I will skip over forty-five years of Shakyamuni's teachings and focus on the time just before he passed away, that is, the enlightenment or state of Shakyamuni at the age of eighty, by writing out his inner voice.

Under sal trees in Kushinagar, Shakyamuni Buddha laid on his right side, with his right arm folded under his head and his left hand on his ailing stomach. As he was about to enter nirvana, he was thinking what follows.

"Ever since I attained enlightenment at the age of thirty-five, for forty-five years, I explored goodness and taught what the Right Principles are. But now the time has come for me to leave my physical body. Oh, my physical body which has become feeble with age, everything in this world is transient. I have no attachment to you, whatsoever. Indeed, for more than forty years, the way to Buddha that I taught and the way human beings should live that I have shown are the Laws, which are indeed my true body.

"Ah, my disciples, you did very well for so many years. You worked very hard from attending to my personal needs to spreading the Laws. Thanks to your efforts, my order has become a large religious group with more than five thousand renunciant monks. There are also hundreds of thousands of people, a countless number, who follow my teachings throughout India. This is all thanks to your continuous efforts in spreading the Laws, even as you fought against religious persecution or cleverly avoided the enemies of the Truth. If it were not for your help, my Laws would not have spread so far. Keep working just as diligently as you have been doing without neglecting your duties.

"Sariputra, you passed away a few years ago, and I am leaving this world soon, so I will see you again. We can enjoy another of our talks, face to face. You were such a great help to me. As the best in wisdom, you were always a good listener, and you made it easy for me to preach. Your odd questions at times made me smile wryly, but who knows how much you were appreciated by the people who didn't have the courage to ask me questions.

"Mahamaudgalyayana, although I knew it was part of your spiritual discipline to persevere, I was unable to hold back my tears when I heard that you, known as the best in divine powers, had been attacked and murdered by followers of a misguided religion. I can see you coming on a shining cloud to take me up.

"Mahakatyayana, you, the best at debating, were always able to explain my teachings in ways that others could understand. You will continue to sow the seeds of the Dharma in remote areas after I am gone. Spread my teachings in Avanti and its surrounding areas in west India.

"Subhuti, you, the best at understanding void, never became attached to material things, and gained a deep understanding of my teachings on egolessness and void. May you continue your diligent efforts.

"Aniruddha, you once fell asleep during one of my lectures, so I unusually scolded you harshly. Then, you meditated night and day, until you became blind. Fortunately, you have learned to see through your spiritual eyes, becoming known as the best in tengen. You were once so young and pure, but it looks like you have grown gray.

"Purnamaitrayaniputra, from the Shakya clan, you are very clever, enough to be called the best at preaching the Dharma. You and the other Purna, who plans to travel west to spread my teachings, will become good rivals.

"Mahakasyapa, you will not see my passing and will arrive here at Kushinagar a week later. You will be furious with Ananda, who carelessly served me poisonous mushrooms and so hurried me to death. You will try to expel him from the order and will cry uncontrollably over my death. You, known as the best in spiritual discipline, were always meticulous about the methods of religious practice. But after my death, you may do away with petty precepts.

"Upali, you were the best in observing the rules. You have always tried to do your work with great care, and you were courteous to everyone you met. Although you were from a lower caste, you remained undaunted and devoted yourself to spiritual discipline among others who were of aristocratic origin. You did well.

"Rahula, although you were my real son, you strived to train privately under Sariputra. As a result, you were called the best in hidden training, but you left this world much too early. You were expected to succeed me, and it was very unfortunate to lose you so soon. I could not do anything for you as a father, but I wonder if you are living happily over there.

"Jivaka, the best and famous doctor, you have cured my illnesses many times, but this time there was nothing you could do. All things are transient. Just as you cannot stop the flow of a river, you cannot extend my life on earth any longer.

"Ah, when I think of you, my beloved disciples, I cannot stop thinking about what will happen to you after I leave this world. My disciples, remember this well: although I will be leaving this world shortly, the teachings I am leaving behind will be passed on for thousands of years to serve as nourishment for people's souls.

"My eternal disciples, remember my last words well. My life is like the full moon. Clouds may cover the moon and hide it from you, but it indeed continues to shine its brilliance behind the clouds. Likewise, life shines eternally; it never comes to an end.

"From now on, even after I have left this world, keep living with the teachings I have given you over the past forty-five years as nourishment for your souls. With my teachings as the nourishment for your soul, light up your own mind by yourself, illuminating your way ahead without others having to light it up for you. Light the torch of Dharma within you, and live unwaveringly.

"The teachings I have taught you over many, many years are the teachings to cultivate yourself; they are also the teachings to save others while you cultivate yourself. Even after my passing, never forget to light your inner torch, and live with the Dharma as your guide. My disciples, these are my last words. *All things in this world will pass. Without slacking, complete your discipline.*"

These were the thoughts of Shakyamuni Buddha as he passed away. In his last moments, even the great Shakyamuni Buddha could hardly speak but some disciples whose windows of the mind were open were able to hear his inner voice through their spiritual power. Some of what they heard was later recorded in the Nirvana Sutra.

10

The Enlightenment of the Ninth Dimension

Shakyamuni's level of enlightenment surpassed that attained by Jesus Christ and was the highest level of enlightenment of humankind. Unfortunately, however, even after spending forty-five years teaching his disciples, Shakyamuni Buddha could not fully pass on the enlightenment about the great universe that he attained. Even though they were his disciples, hardly any of them attained the enlightenment of tathagata while alive, so most of them found it difficult to understand how the great universe was created or understand its multidimensional structure. What is more, India in those days was in constant war. In such a situation, Shakyamuni would not have been able to save people's minds by teaching something that was very much advanced for their time. This is why Shakyamuni focused on the teachings to raise people's awareness to the state of arhat through the Eightfold Path.

In essence, the enlightenment of the ninth dimensional Cosmic Realm must fulfill the following three conditions.

1. To be awakened to the Laws from every perspective and be able to preach them in a way that is suited to all people.

2. To also be awakened to Creation, that is to say, how the universe came to be and the history of Earth.

3. To be awakened to the laws of the multidimensional world of the fourth dimension and higher.

As for the first condition, Shakyamuni excelled at preaching the Truth in a way that was well suited to each person. As for the second condition, he awakened to Creation when he attained enlightenment under a bodhi tree and had the mystical experience of his spirit body becoming one with the great universe. As for the third condition, in other words, the laws of the universe or the rules of the Real World, he expressed them in his teachings of the law of cause and effect and the law of karma.

Of course, with the enlightenment of the ninth dimension come all of the six divine supernatural powers of the highest level, as well as the ability to see through past, present, and future lives. However, at an early stage Shakyamuni already understood the danger of seekers of Truth becoming obsessed with supernatural powers and, in order to prevent people from falling into delusional beliefs, he did not use spiritual powers very much, with the exception of mind reading.

In Chapter One, I mentioned that there are 10 great guiding spirits of light who have attained the enlightenment of the ninth dimension, a very high realm of the Spirit World. Here are their current roles (as of 1994):

(Front Heaven)

1. Shakyamuni (El Cantare)
To create a new era and build a new civilization.
The highest grand spirit of the Earth Spirit Group.

2. Jesus Christ (Amor)
To decide the guiding policies of the heavenly world.

3. Confucius (Therabim)
To design the evolution of the Earth Spirit Group. Interacts
with other star clusters.

4. Manu
To deal with ethnic issues.

5. Maitreya
To disperse Buddha's light in many ways.

6. Newton
Science and technology.

7. Zeus
Arts, such as music, fine art and literature.

8. Zoroaster
Moral perfection.

(Rear Heaven)

9. Moses (Moria)

To command the forces dedicated to the dissolution of Hell; also to bring about miraculous phenomena.

10. Enlil

To guide the Sorcery Realm (Arabia), the Yoga Realm (India), the Sennin Realm (China), and the Sennin and Tengu Realms (Japan). (Belongs to the line of harsh gods and gods of vengeance.)

The core consciousness of El Cantare is now present on earth, so in the ninth dimension, Jesus Christ is the main decision maker in place of El Cantare. It is planned for Jesus Christ to descend again in about 400 years. By then, the ocean floor where the current Bermuda Triangle is located will resurface, forming the New Atlantis continent which will include the current location of Canada. The southern half of what is currently North America will have sunk beneath the ocean. For now, it is planned that Jesus will be reborn in the New Atlantis continent. There, he is expected to preach the Truth mainly based on the principles of love and justice for the new space age.

In this chapter, I have covered up to the enlightenment of the ninth dimension, but of course, above this is the enlightenment of the tenth dimension. The consciousnesses in the tenth dimension are three planetary consciousnesses—

Grand Sun Consciousness, Moon Consciousness, and Earth Consciousness, but if we define enlightenment to be that of spirits that are able to reside in a human body, then we can leave out the enlightenment of the tenth dimension. In addition, if I were to state the enlightenment of the tenth dimension, it is enlightenment with all human elements removed. That is to say, the beings in the tenth dimension are solely gigantic masses of light that have consciousness with purpose.

ENDNOTES

1 Rojin refers to an ability to get rid of all worldly desires; it is the power of higher wisdom, rather than simply a supernatural power. Daily practice of self-reflection is indispensable to become free of all worldly desires. Rojin enables you to lead a normal secular life while possessing high-level supernatural powers.

2 Primordial Buddha refers to Lord El Cantare. Here, it denotes the soul parent of Shakyamuni Buddha.

CHAPTER FIVE

THE
GOLDEN
AGES

1

Signs of a New Humankind

We are in the second half of the twentieth century, and the twenty-first century is just ahead of us. What kind of people will we see and what kind of age will we see in the coming era? Many people today may be excited or feel nervous about the twenty-first century, filled with either hope or uncertainty. But the indications of a new age and signs of a new humankind to come are already in today's society. Now is a time of transition. In a time of transition, many old things perish and many new things emerge. So, the buds of the new era are already here in the current time. To tell these things to the people of today is the mission of a prophet born in this same era.

About 10,000 years ago, humanity witnessed an older civilization perish when the continent of Atlantis sank. The end of something is the beginning of another. Then, a new civilization eventually developed, starting mainly in the land of Egypt. This civilization has lasted for about 10,000 years, and the final years of the twentieth century will mark its end.

For the last 10,000 years, the current civilization has flourished in many countries and regions, starting in Egypt and then moving to Persia, Judea, China, Europe, America, and Japan. It can be said that the distinctive feature of this civilization is intelligence; it is an age with a very strong emphasis on intelligence. So, it is a civilization of intelligence, where people are heavily inclined to try to understand the world intellectually.

Before this, the civilization on the continent of Atlantis mainly focused on reason, and Maitreya Tathagata and Koot Hoomi (Koot Hoomi was later born as Archimedes and then as Newton) played very active roles in the ninth dimensional Cosmic Realm at that time.

In the age before Atlantis, more than 15,000 years ago, there was the continent called Mu in the Pacific Ocean, and it also had its own civilization. In short, the Mu civilization was a civilization of light energy. The people of Mu were very advanced in scientific research and spiritual research regarding light energy, and their spiritual training was mainly about learning how each person could amplify the power of his or her own light energy.

And going back further, more than 27,000 years ago, there was the continent called Ramudia[1] in the Indian Ocean. The people in those times mainly focused on developing their senses. While there was great influence from the power of El Cantare (Shakyamuni Buddha) during the age of Mu, it was Manu and Zeus who exerted their power during the age of Ramudia. They played central roles in shaping the civilization of the senses. In those times, people focused their discipline to refine their senses, and the most accomplished people were capable of distinguishing 3,000 colors and 2,500 smells.

And even before the Ramudia civilization was the Myutram civilization. It flourished on the continent of Myutram that disappeared long ago, 153,000 years back. In those times, the Earth's axis was in a very different position compared to that of today. The continent of Antarctica today, which previously had a temperate climate and a slightly different shape, was then called the Myutram continent. Unlike the Mu continent or the Atlantis continent, this continent did not disappear by sinking into the sea. Actually, about 150,000 years ago, when the Earth's axis shifted, the continent's climate changed from warm to frigid. As a result, the land became covered in ice, causing almost all the people and other living things to perish. The story of this occurrence has been handed down in the account of the Ice Age. Many traces of this old civilization still remain under the Antarctic ice.

Before the Myutram continent, there was the Garna continent[2], which existed around 735,000 years ago. In those times, what are now the African and South American continents were still connected as one huge land mass. The Garna civilization was a civilization mainly focused on supernatural powers. But one day, pulled by the sudden movement of the Earth's crust, the land split in two, and began to shift apart. The Garna civilization was hit by a great earthquake of about Magnitude 10 and was destroyed.

What I am telling you here is not science fiction. They are things that actually happened on Earth in the past. They can be helpful when thinking about today's civilization and future civilizations.

2

The Garna Civilization

In the 400-million-year history of humankind, countless civilizations have emerged, then to disappear like bubbles floating down a river. But it is not necessary to talk to the people of today about them all. For now, what we need are references to think about the present and future societies. We need to check if such references are buried in past civilizations. So, I decided to look into the Akashic Records in the Real World and tell you briefly about the transition of the civilizations of the last one million years, which is only a small part of the 400-million-year history.

First, I will explain the Garna civilization. The continent of Garna rose from the sea 962,000 years ago after an underwater volcanic eruption caused the seabed to rise. It was located in the area between the present-day African and South American continents. But about 735,000 years ago, an unprecedented event occurred which caused the continent to split and move apart; one continent became two continents.

Four civilizations were built on the Garna continent, but here, I will focus only on the final one and call it the Garna civilization. The Garna civilization flourished for approximately 25,000 years from around 760,000 years ago to the end of the continent. As I said earlier, this civilization was mainly focused on supernatural powers. At that time the average height of men was 2.1 meters (7 feet) and the average height of women was 1.8 meters (6 feet). These were the standard heights. Interestingly, the men in that age had a third eye. An emerald-greenish, round eye was located in the center of the forehead, approximately two centimeters (0.8 inch) above the eyebrows. This third eye was usually closed, and opened only when the supernatural power was used. Women did not have the third eye, so were very afraid of men's third eye of supernatural powers, which resulted in a subservient position for them.

The myth told near the end of the Garna civilization was that, "God created men and women equally. As proof of that, God gave men a third eye to protect themselves and their kind, while women were given a womb for the prosperity of their kind." In those times, a woman's womb was also considered an organ of supernatural power because it allowed women to communicate with the heavenly world and choose the spirits of the children-to-be their bodies would bear. Women would discuss deeply with them who were in the heavenly world. When they reached a mutual agreement, the spirits were conceived. So, unlike in our times, abortions would never happen.

In further detail, during the age of the Garna civilization, eight tribes were fighting for supremacy, so people needed to protect themselves from outside enemies all the time. The third eye was a weapon to help them do this. The color of the third eye varied depending on the tribe—it could be yellow, green, purple, black, gray, or brown. The type and the degree of development of the supernatural powers were different depending on the tribe, and the most dominant power of the third eye was the ability to affect physical objects. However, some tribes developed the ability of precognition. In short, they tried to protect their kind by sensing outside enemy attacks using precognitive ability before they could take place.

Unfortunately, the Truth during this age lacked the teaching of the mind. People's main concern was the type of supernatural powers they wanted to exert, and their spiritual training was about how to attain them. With the vanishing of the Garna continent, these people returned to the other world and this increased the numbers of inhabitants in the Sennin Realm, Tengu Realm, and Sorcery Realm (Sennin Realm of the West) in Rear Heaven.

There has been no race with a third eye since the Garna civilization. But the chakra between the eyebrows, as referred to in yoga, is a trace of the third eye.

3

The Myutram Civilization

The Garna civilization focused mainly on supernatural powers, and it was eventually destroyed after an unprecedented event tore the continent into two. It happened one autumn evening, about 735,000 years ago. With thunderous underground rumbling, a crack opened running north and south, right through the center of Ecarna, a large city that was one of the major cities of the Garna civilization. Before long, a massive rift was formed. At first, the rift was about a hundred kilometers (60 miles) long from north to south, but as seawater began to surge in, signs that the continent would split started to show. The second change happened three days later, when a great earthquake of about Magnitude 10 shook the land; the epicenter was located right below the city. About 300,000 people living in Ecarna perished that day. The north-south crack then grew to several thousand miles long and the Garna continent slowly split in two. Over the next tens of thousands of years, the land masses evolved into how they are today—the continents of Africa and South America.

In the southeastern part of Garna, there was a city called Emilna. Members of the tribe living mainly in Emilna were particularly developed in foreseeing the future, so some of them were able to quickly foresee the catastrophe, and they escaped by ship to an uninhabited, new continent in the south. This event was one of the origins that later developed into the story of Noah's Ark. However, the Emilna tribe lost the advanced tools they once had, as well as many of their great people. As a result, they gradually regressed into simple, agricultural people. As they did, the third eye I mentioned earlier also began to degenerate.

Many civilizations would come to be built on this new continent, and the most famous one was called the Myutram civilization which flourished from 300,000 to about 153,000 years ago. The continent was called Myutram after the name of this civilization. Eighty percent of the continent overlapped with present-day Antarctica, but since the position of the Earth's axis at that time was very different from its position today, unlike the Antarctica of today the continent had a warm climate. So, food grains very similar to wheat could be bountifully harvested, and a civilization based on agriculture was built.

The Myutram civilization was especially developed in the research of dietary lifestyle. In this age people studied all aspects of dietary life extensively. They thoroughly researched the relationship between dietary and spiritual life to see what combination of foods were most beneficial to human nature. What kinds of vegetables would cultivate a gentle disposition? What kinds of fish would improve muscle response? How much and how many times of which dairy products should be consumed daily to extend one's lifespan? What type of alcohol would help the brain cells become more active? Things like these were studied. There were specialists in each field of dietary culture, for example, experts in longevity, endurance, and memory enhancement. Although different from the entrance exam studies done today, children would study hard to become experts in these subjects.

The Myutram civilization produced a large volume of research on the relationship between dietary lifestyle and human temperament. Unfortunately, in contrast to the Garna civilization, which despite an aggressive nature placed a high value on spiritual powers, the Myutram civilization was peaceful but there was an underlying tendency to think lightly of spirituality. Thus, early forms of the materialism we see today had already begun to appear at that time. Although the civilization's discoveries of the relationship between diet and human character were important, this main focus on dietary life caused the Myutram culture to neglect the true mission of human beings—to explore and train the soul. Some people today who have an avid interest in a healthy diet or a beauty diet were most likely born several times in the Myutram civilization and worked on that type of research.

The Myutram civilization reached its peak around 160,000 years ago when Moria, known as Great Teacher Emula at the time, initiated a grand-scale spiritual revolution with the slogan, "From dietary life to mind-based life." But Great Teacher Emula was persecuted harshly for disrespecting the importance of Myutram's culture of dietary life, which was part of its tradition. His spiritual revolution therefore did not succeed. Nevertheless, he was able to imprint upon people's minds the idea that, "there are some other things, besides just dietary life, that greatly affect human nature." In a way, this idea was a forerunner of modern religious movements that are fighting against materialism.

Then, 153,000 years ago, a sudden polar shift occurred, and the climate on the continent of Myutram became frigid. This was the beginning of the Ice Age.

4

The Ramudia Civilization

The end of the Myutram civilization was caused by a shift in the Earth's axis. One evening during sunset, 153,000 years ago, people noticed that the sky was unusually red. The whole sky was red as if it were coated in blood. Experts were flooded with inquiries, but no one could provide an explanation for the phenomenon. Then, at around ten o'clock that night, people saw all the stars slide position in the sky. But people soon realized that they were not shooting stars. It was the Earth that was moving, not the stars. In the same way that a ball released underwater spins after it shoots up to the surface, the Earth spun and changed its position.

The effect of this phenomenon showed clearly on earth within a few months; snow began to fall on the once temperate lands of Myutram and the ground began to freeze. This phenomenon was fatal for Myutram, a civilization based on agriculture. Soon after, people began to suffer from starvation. Some even tried building cities underground to survive, but they also perished in just two to three years. Unfortunately, it was the rainy season at the time, so the constant rain turned to snow and it accumulated to more than five meters (16 feet) in height in about two weeks. The capital city of Myutram, Ra Myute, was completely destroyed at that time. But some of its people managed to escape on ships. So, some of the Myutram civilization was able to continue on to the next continent.

In those times there were no large continents in the region that is now the Indian Ocean, but only a small island about twice the size of Japan. Several thousand refugees from Myutram settled there and their numbers grew steadily. But around 86,000 years ago, this island suddenly began to rise and eventually a continent was formed in the Indian Ocean. In about a year's time, this massive continent, Ramudia, took full shape. It was indeed the largest continent to ever rise out of the ocean; a rhombus of land that stretched 3,500 kilometers (2,200 miles) east and west and 4,700 kilometers (2,900 miles) north and south. Eventually, abundant vegetation grew on Ramudia and it became a fertile land.

And about 44,000 years ago, the one who would later be born in Greece as Zeus appeared in Ramudia. His name at the time was not Zeus, but Elemaria. Elemaria was a genius in all aspects of art, including literature, fine arts, and music. Through art, Great Saint Elemaria taught people the joy of living and the glory of God. So, after Elemaria, the Ramudia civilization flourished greatly in the fields of music, painting, literature, poetry, architecture, sculpture and the like. Many people of today who excel in arts most probably were hard at work in the age of Ramudia.

The one who brought enormous light upon Ramudia after Great Saint Elemaria was Manu. Manu was born in Ramudia about 29,000 years ago. At that time, he was given the name Margarit; he was called Great Teacher Margarit. His name meant "one who rises to compete," which had two meanings. One was that he competed with Great Saint Elemaria, who had then already been worshipped as an omnipotent god, and the other was that Margarit let the tribes vie against one another in artistic competition.

Manu, or Great Teacher Margarit, was the first person to introduce the principle of competition in art. He divided his people into five groups according to different fields of art—music, painting, literature, architecture, and craftsmanship—and encouraged all to aim for the best in their own field. Every three years he held competitions to determine which group had produced the finest art overall, and the winning group was given the prize of being the country's ruling class for the next three years.

Although this system was limited to the arts, the method of selecting rulers through fair public contests became the forerunner of modern democracy. What's more, Margarit taught that ultimate art leads to God, so his teachings aimed to unite religion and politics. However, the Ramudia civilization disappeared from the Indian Ocean quite abruptly 27,000 years ago. It happened on a severely hot summer afternoon, as the people indulged themselves in music.

5

The Mu Civilization

The end of the Ramudia civilization happened in sudden sequence. It was common practice for the people of Ramudia, who were masters of the arts, to enjoy a two-hour session of music every afternoon. Trembling began just as people were having their musical entertainment. Chandeliers swayed violently, all the glass windows shattered, and shortly after Ramudia's magnificent modern concert halls collapsed. The continent began to sink from its eastern end.

By four o'clock in the afternoon, the continent had already become half its former size. By seven o'clock the following morning, all that was left was the morning sun shining upon the vast blue ocean; not a single trace of the continent remained. A variety of debris was floating in the Indian Ocean, that's all. The destruction of Ramudia was total and awful; its entire population of 2.5 million vanished into the sea without any survivors. Regardless of whether people were good or bad, everyone disappeared. However, the civilization itself survived because the people of Ramudia had established a colony on the continent named Moa, which later came to be known as Mu.

Mu was a continent in the Pacific Ocean. It appeared long before the Ramudia continent, some 370,000 years ago. Continental Mu changed into different shapes over time, and near the end of Ramudia, it was approximately twice the size of present-day Australia with its center close to where Indonesia is today. Although people had lived on this continent for hundreds of thousands of years before that time, they lived rather simply. Most people in the north were fishers, most in the south were hunters, and most in the midwest were farmers.

However, as the civilization in Ramudia flourished, the Mu people were eventually invaded by the Ramudia people. Around 28,000 years ago, the Ramudia people had sent a large fleet of big sailing ships to the Mu continent and began colonization of various cities. They took the people of Mu back to Ramudia as slaves, and had them do menial work, while they themselves spent their days enjoying their studies and the arts. Such disharmonious thought-energy was cast over Ramudia like a massive dark cloud toward the end of its civilization that, as a reaction, the continent would later sink. As Mu was a colony of Ramudia, the culture of Ramudia began to take root on the Mu continent. After the Ramudia civilization perished, signs of a civilization slowly but surely began to appear on the Mu continent.

About 20,000 years ago, one of the past lives of Zoroaster descended to the land of Mu. His name at the time was Escallent. The word *excellent* in current use originated from his name and they both have the same meaning. Great Saint Escallent focused on the scientific aspect of solar energy. He devised two teachings about the power of sunlight; first, that light was something sacred representing God's glory, and second, he evaluated the useful importance of light.

In accordance to the first point, light being sacred, a tradition was developed where people would always put their hands together and bow down on one knee whenever they first saw a source of light, whether it be the sun, the moon, or an indoor lamp. This custom became the source of bowing in later Oriental culture.

According to the second point, light was something useful, but what did this mean? With guidance from Koot Hoomi (who was later born as Archimedes and Newton) and others in the heavenly world, and Enlil regarding scientific way of thinking, Escallent focused on amplifying the power of light. People of his time would use gigantic solar energy amplifiers as power generators for their room lights, to drive their ships, or as energy used to make things. In hindsight, this was when humankind started preparing for the age of science.

At the centers of cities were shining silver pyramids of regular triangles measuring 30 meters (100 feet) each side. The solar energy which these pyramids absorbed was amplified before being relayed to smaller pyramids in every town of 10-meter (30-foot) size. These pyramids supplied the energy to even smaller pyramids, one meter (three feet) long on each side, that were on the rooftops of all houses. This pyramid-power was passed down to the Atlantis civilization, which came later on. The gigantic solar energy amplifiers of the time worked in a very similar way to what is now called pyramid-power.

6

The Age of Ra Mu

The Mu continent reached its peak during the age of Ra Mu. That is, close to 17,000 years ago. At that time, Mu was experiencing an age where worship of the sun and solar technology were at their height. During that age, Ra Mu was born into a physical body. Ra Mu was a past life of Shakyamuni Buddha, several lives before. Ra Mu means "Great King of Light of Mu." A great empire was established on Continental Mu in the age of Ra Mu. It was previously called the Moa continent, but during the age of Ra Mu, it was renamed the Mu continent and the civilization was renamed the Mu civilization after Ra Mu.

Ra Mu was pleased to see the scientific civilization on the Mu continent greatly advancing, and thought that the time to build a kingdom of God was then or never. Ra Mu himself had great spiritual powers, so he was of course able to freely communicate with the spirits in the heavenly world. At that time, the spirit guarding Ra Mu from the heavenly world was mainly Amor, who would later be born as Jesus Christ.

Ra Mu's teachings were centered on three points. First, all the people of Mu were to awaken to the idea that God was like the sun. God is full of light, giving light to all of us on earth just like the sun. Second, all people of Mu were to live with love and mercy, just like the sun. How much did they fill other's minds with bright light? This was the true nature of love and mercy. Third, all the people of Mu were to set self-development as their life goal. Development did not only apply to studies, the arts, and martial arts, but above all to how they were able to refine their spirituality. These three points were the basis of Ra Mu's teachings. Taking into account that Ra Mu was a past life of Shakyamuni Buddha, who spread Buddhism in India about 14,000 years later, we can see that the teachings of Buddhism were already beginning to appear during the age of Ra Mu.

Ra Mu's teachings, given 17,000 years ago, marked the starting point of real religion. During the age of Ra Mu, religion and politics were never separated. The best religion meant the best politics, and the greatest religious leader meant the greatest politician. When we think about it, this makes perfect sense; since human beings branched off from God, it is only natural that the one closest to God, in other words, a great religious leader, should govern people on earth.

Every night, Ra Mu would kneel in his shrine and spiritually communicate with the high spirits, asking for their opinion regarding basic national policies. This was indeed the starting point of politics. The reason is, politics is the art of governing people, and if a ruler makes a mistake, it will not only be his or her problem alone, but will also endanger the lives of all citizens and will lead their souls to downfall. To make such important judgments based purely on human thoughts could be seen as very arrogant and extremely conceited. This is where the starting point of politics is—to humble oneself before God, and to listen to God with a calm and selfless mind. It is to listen carefully to the words of God.

However, after Ra Mu passed away and people were no longer influenced by his great teachings, the golden age of the Mu civilization began to decline. People denied the power of enlightenment and a strange worship of animal spirits began to spread in many places. People with wrong faith in spiritual power ridiculed the teachings of love and mercy and caused dark clouds of thought energy to cover the whole continent.

Because of this, about 15,300 years ago, the Mu continent sank into the ocean in three stages. Of course, when the continent sank, the large and advanced metropolitan city of Ra Mu, which was named after Ra Mu himself, sank into the Pacific Ocean. But some people of Mu somehow managed to escape. Among them, some headed north by ship and became ancestors of the Vietnamese, Japanese, and Chinese. Others who traveled east across the Pacific Ocean went on to live in the mountains of the Andes in South America. There were also people who were able to escape to the Atlantic Ocean, in search of new land, and reached the Atlantis continent.

7

The Atlantis Civilization

The Atlantis civilization was the civilization right before the one of today. In the middle of what is now the Atlantic Ocean, mainly around the Bermuda Triangle, there used to be a continent called Atlantis. It was an island about the size of Great Britain until a huge underwater volcanic eruption around 75,000 years ago lifted the land up out of the ocean. The continent's first residents appeared about 42,000 years ago. At that time, they were still an underdeveloped people; they had migrated there from neighboring islands to settle there.

Signs of a civilization on Atlantis appeared about 16,000 years ago, a few hundred years before the Mu continent sank. Around that time, the soul of a great scientist, who later incarnated in Greece as Archimedes, was born with the name Koot Hoomi. He initiated the first civilization for the people there who had been living there mainly by hunting and fishing.

Koot Hoomi noticed the mystical power that was possessed by plant life. Why did a seed sprout, grow a stem, develop leaves, and bloom into flowers? Why did bulbs grow stems? He spent about 20 years studying these things.

Eventually, he discovered the essence of life's energy. He found that life itself was a treasury of energy and when it changed form, it involved a huge amount of energy conversion. He then thought that if the power from this energy conversion could be extracted, it could be used as a power source for various things. He spent the next decade searching for a way to extract the conversion power of life energy, and succeeded. This became the driving force of the civilization.

Ever since Koot Hoomi discovered this power source, a new light began to shine on Atlantis. This life energy conversion power was used in the same way as electricity is used today, and objects similar to electrical appliances appeared. For example, every house had many flasks containing plant bulbs lined up by a window. A machine that was connected to the plant bulbs by something unique which looked like a nichrome wire would extract the energy the plant bulbs produced when they sprouted, and transfer it to another machine above to amplify the energy. This is how each household secured the energy it needed.

However, a major change occurred about 15,300 years ago when the Mu continent sank and some of its survivors escaped to Atlantis. There were scientists among them and they passed down the pyramid-power of the Mu civilization to the Atlantis people.

Around the same time, Maitreya Tathagata was born into a physical body from the heavenly world. His name at the time was Cusanus. Saint Cusanus began to teach a kind of deism which was a faith that combined pyramid-power and sun worship. According to this philosophy, rational and scientific things were in accordance with God's Will, and God's Will expected things to be rational and scientific. The best example of this was the light of the sun. "The light of the sun benefits humankind scientifically through pyramid-power and, furthermore, benefits them spiritually in that it teaches God's Will. The light of the sun is such a wonderful thing." This was the main teaching of Maitreya's deism. Pyramid-power was later used in aviation and navigation technologies.

The Atlantis civilization reached its peak about 12,000 years ago under the great religious master or great leader, Omniscient and Omnipotent Lord Thoth. Thoth was a super genius who was a religious leader, politician, philosopher, scientist, and artist all in one. This great leader established what may be called a multi-faceted culture in Atlantis. He was particularly gifted in scientific insight, and as a result, Atlantis built a scientific civilization unattained by the Mu civilization. Namely, airship and submarine technologies developed through pyramid-power.

The airships of Atlantis were shaped in a very unusual manner. They were whale-shaped about four meters (13 feet) in diameter and about 30 meters (100 feet) long. The upper half of the airship contained gas to make it float and the lower half could hold about 20 people. On the top were mounted three silver pyramids that looked like dorsal fins which converted solar energy to drive the propeller attached at the rear. The airships of Atlantis mainly flew on sunny days. Commercial flights were canceled on rainy days.

There were also submarines. They were four meters (13 feet) wide and 20 meters (66 feet) long, made of alloys, and shaped to resemble orcas. The orca was the symbol of Atlantis. And although it has been said that Atlantis was named after a king called Atlas, the word *atlantis* also means "shining golden orca." The submarines were also fitted with three pyramids that looked like dorsal fins from afar. Whenever they surfaced, they absorbed solar energy before diving again. This is how Atlantis entered this age of their most advanced science.

8

The Age of Agasha

After the time of the great master Thoth, Atlantis entered the age of "science almighty." But since there was no leader who was truly almighty like Thoth, people began placing too much importance on science. So, some people began to consider the idea that, "science is everything" was not always in accordance with God's Will and that perhaps God's Will could be found elsewhere. Then, various religious reformers of both large and small scale sprung up to preach how human beings should be. This age was the so-called "age of a hundred schools of thought." It lasted for about a thousand years.

Atlantis began to sink around this time, which was about 11,000 years ago. First, the eastern third of the continent sank into the sea. Then, about 10,700 years ago, the western third sank. The Atlantis continent was left with only its central third above the sea, but even then, the empire thrived.

Then, about 10,400 years ago, some decades before 8,400 B.C., a man named Agasha was born on this land. Agasha was born in Pontis, the capital of Atlantis. Pontis was a city of about 700,000 people. A royal family called the Amanda clan had lived there, and they had ruled down through the generations. Agasha was a prince born into the Amanda clan. His name at birth was Amon. At the age of twenty-four, Amon was crowned king and changed his name to Agasha, which means, "he who treasures wisdom." Great King Agasha was the one who was later born in Israel as Jesus Christ.

Like Ra Mu, Great King Agasha was both a political leader and religious leader. In his palace, he had a 30-meter-high (100-foot-high) golden shrine shaped like a pyramid, and here he performed his religious duties. A unique feature of his reign was that once a month, he would gather citizens in a large open space that could hold more than 100,000 people and preach to them. Even in that time, there was definitely something like the wireless microphone that is used today.

Agasha's teachings were mainly based on love, which is understandable given he was later born as Jesus. Although the lecture content was different every time, his basic teachings can be summarized into the following four points.

1. The essence of God is love, and the proof that we are children of God is the love in all of our minds.

2. The precise way of practicing love is to first love the Lord God, then love one's neighbors, who are branches of God, and finally to love oneself, a servant of God.

3. At least once a day, pray peacefully on your own and communicate with your guardian and guiding spirits.

4. The greatness of human beings is measured not by the quantity of love, but by the quality of love that he or she gives, so one must raise the quality of one's love.

Agasha's teachings were respectable and he, as a person, was deeply revered by his people. However, one sect which was devoted to the deist teachings of Saint Cusanus (Maitreya Tathagata) considered Agasha an enemy and sought his death. This was because while Saint Cusanus taught that God was rational and placed great emphasis on science and logic, Agasha preached non-scientific, illogical, and irrational teachings such as love and the existence of guardian and guiding spirits. In short, believers of Saint Cusanus thought that Agasha's teachings led people astray and would gradually weaken the conventional traditions of Atlantis.

Agasha was surely an extraordinary figure and the nobleness of his character was acknowledged by everyone, but the common people of Atlantis were of the belief that science was almighty, and they could not believe in guardian and guiding spirits that were unable to be seen with their own eyes. Eventually, the deists rebelled and committed an outrage by capturing Agasha and the royal family, and buried them alive in the city square. Devils became fierce as the Truth was being taught, just like they have in today's society at the end of the twentieth century.

During this violence, one person was able to escape the attack of the deists by taking flight from the palace alone in an airship. It was Amon II, Agasha's first son. He escaped to Egypt and became the source of Amon-Ra in ancient Egyptian myth. He started sun worship in that land. The original form of the Egyptian pyramids came from the knowledge passed down by Amon II.

Many angels of light born on earth with physical bodies were executed as a result of the rampage of the rebels, making it seem as if the devils had won in Atlantis. However, the dark clouds of evil thought energy that they produced covered all Atlantis, making Earth Consciousness react, and the whole Atlantean Empire was caused to sink to the bottom of the ocean in just a single day. People witnessed such an unbelievable phenomenon.

Like many civilizations before it, the Atlantis civilization was ended by the sudden sinking of the continent. But once again, some of the people escaped in airships to Africa, Spain, and the Andes in South America, and went on to plant seeds of new civilizations in each land.

9

The Transitions in Modern Civilization

After the collapse of Atlantis, civilizations spread all over the world in different forms. First, Amon II, who fled to Egypt, was worshipped as a deity there and taught people about having faith in the light. He also taught the Egyptians, who were living mainly by raising crops and livestock, various kinds of wisdom with which to build a civilization. The pyramids that were built later were modeled after a private pyramid which Amon-Ra had built earlier for himself to worship. Later, in Egypt, one of the past lives of Jesus Christ, Clario, appeared. This was four thousand and some hundreds of years ago. At that time, Clario guided people on the basis combining faith in the sun and faith in love.

Meanwhile, on the South American continent, descendants of Mu and Atlantis were working together to build their own unique civilization. These people, believing that beings from outer space were gods exalted communication with such beings so as to be the core of their civilization. They even built a base where flying craft could take off and land in the mountains of the Andes, so that beings from outer space could travel there. The people were preoccupied with that for a period of time.

However, about 7,000 years ago, a king named Rient Arl Croud was born among the ancient Inca in the Andes mountains. He declared that beings from outer space were not gods. He taught people the mystical nature of the world of the mind, stating that God was not found outside of us, but in the depths of our minds. He also taught that the purpose of human life was to explore the mysteries of the world of the mind, and that it was important to bring oneself closer to God by elevating the mind.

Rient Arl Croud was actually an incarnation of the energy form of Ra Mu on the Mu continent and Thoth of Atlantis. This energy form would later preach the Dharma in India as Gautama Siddhartha, or Shakyamuni Buddha. Unlike human souls of the fourth dimension or fifth dimension, souls of the ninth dimension are massive bodies of light energy, so it is more accurate to say that a part of the same energy form comes down to earth than to say that the same soul is born again. It is therefore the same with Jesus.

Moving on, about 3,700 or 3,800 years ago, Zeus appeared in the land we now call Greece. As proof of his later being called "the omniscient and omnipotent," he excelled in both studies and the arts. As Zeus was in charge of the arts in general in the ninth dimension, he started a beautiful culture in Greece. The distinctive feature of his teachings was setting the human nature free. He was wary of how religion made people suffer by making them feel sinful, so instead he put his energy into cultivating a bright and relaxed human nature. That is why the gods of Greek mythology are so bright and full of joy.

Furthermore, about 3,200 or 3,300 years ago, Moses was born in Egypt. He was born as the son of a slave, and was set adrift in a reed basket. He was fortunately found and raised in the royal palace. When he got older, Moses, who discovered that he was the son of a slave, eventually led hundreds of thousands of people in an exodus across the Red Sea to Canaan. Moses received various revelations from God, such as the famous Ten Commandments.

Then Jesus Christ appeared 2,000 years ago from among the Israelites. Jesus preached the teachings of love, was eventually crucified, then later resurrected and appeared before his disciples. His resurrection was actually the materialization of his spirit body, but in order for his disciples to accept his resurrection, he showed them that he could eat and do other things. It became apparent that the resurrection of Jesus was not of the physical body. His ascension also clarified this.

While Jesus had been receiving guidance from more than one spirit in the heavenly world, Hermes was in charge of guiding him on his core teachings of love and faith and his resurrection. The reason Christianity became a world religion in later times was because Jesus practically abandoned faith in the ancient Jewish god of vengeance (faith in Yahweh) and believed in the God of Love (El Cantare). Even so, it was the god of vengeance who caused Jesus to be crucified. Nevertheless, it can be said that the elevation of Jesus from a mere prophet to the Christ (Savior) and the spread of his teachings throughout the Roman Empire and Europe in later generations was largely due to the power of Hermes and his group of Greek gods.

Meanwhile, in the East, over 2,500 years ago, Shakyamuni Buddha taught Buddhism in India and furthermore, Confucius taught Confucianism in China. In this way, the seeds of the Laws were sown in places across the world and came to shape the current civilization.

10

Toward the Golden Age

As we look back on the history of civilizations in the last million years or so that lead up to our current civilization, we notice that they had several traits in common. The following are the five common traits.

1. A civilization always has its rise and fall.

2. God (or Buddha) always sent the great guiding spirits of light of the highest level to each civilization.

3. During the peak of a civilization when light was at its brightest, evil became fierce. When humankind was covered with clouds of dark thought-energy, massive catastrophes inevitably occurred, such as the shifting of the Earth's axis or the sinking of a continent.

4. A new civilization inherits the traits of the previous civilization, but always seeks a set of values that are of a different standard.

5. However, no matter what kind of civilization, it served as a necessary training ground for humans to undergo soul training in the process of reincarnation. This is a fact.

If we consider the current civilization in light of these five common traits, we can say that today, the latter half of the twentieth century, closely resembles the Mu and Atlantis civilizations in their final years. Examples of this are that: this age is leaning toward thinking that science is everything and the spread of materialistic thoughts; people's minds are in disharmony and social evils are growing large; and many religious leaders are appearing to lead people astray while sincere religious leaders are also appearing in places around the world.

We can determine what will come in the future by tracing back what happened to past civilizations and by seeing the current state of the modern civilization. We can say that since the current civilization is not on a single continent but spread throughout the world, if natural disasters were to occur, they would happen on a global scale. What's more, it is quite likely that they will occur within the next several decades.

It is easy for me to speak like a prophet based on what I have just mentioned. This is because I can foresee the catastrophes that could occur on Earth as well as the fate of humankind. Yet, I would just like to say this: no matter the scale of confusion, it will not be the end of the world. Such incidents happened in past civilizations, making people think that it was the end of the world, but even so, humankind always built a new paradise of hope or a civilization filled with light.

Just as a human goes through reincarnation, a civilization as a large body of human beings also goes through reincarnation. It means there are births and deaths, in other words, civilizations on

Earth alternate one after another. Therefore, please understand these words well—"The end of one thing is the beginning of another."

I am writing this book, *The Laws of the Sun*, as I receive revelations from the ninth dimension, or Cosmic Realm, precisely because the time when the entire Earth is about to plunge into darkness temporarily is just around the corner. When the world sinks into darkness, we need a lighthouse beam from somewhere. We need the light of Buddha's Truth somewhere. This very book, *The Laws of the Sun*, is the Sun of Buddha's Truth that is now rising and the light for the new civilization that is about to begin.

Humankind will open a new civilization in the twenty-first century after decades of chaos and destruction. And this new civilization will broaden out from Asia. From Japan, it will spread to Southeast Asia, Indonesia, and then to Oceania. Some existing continents will eventually sink into the ocean, but a new Mu continent will surface in the Pacific Ocean where a giant sphere of civilization will be built.

At some point, parts of Europe and America are also planned to sink into the ocean. However, the former Atlantis continent will eventually resurface as an even larger continent. On this land, Jesus Christ is scheduled to be reborn around 2400. Also, around 2800, Moses is scheduled to appear in the flesh and build a new space civilization on the New Garna continent, which is expected to resurface in the Indian Ocean.

Some of you reading this book will probably be reborn during the time of the rebirth of Jesus or Moses and hear their laws. However, the precondition for these civilizations of the future is that we make the Sun of Buddha's Truth rise from Japan. When the world sinks into darkness, Japan will become like the sun and shine. In this sense, you were born in this age, in Japan, with an important mission. Many of those who were once born in the age of Ra Mu, Agasha, Shakyamuni Buddha, or Jesus Christ to help spread Buddha's Truth are now reborn in this country, Japan. A great number of bodhisattvas of light have now been born in Japan. I am sure there are such people among my readers, too.

ENDNOTES

1 In the previous edition, I used the term *Lemuria*, but as some scholars confuse Lemuria with the continent of Mu, I have used the name Ramudia in this edition, which was commonly used at the time that civilization existed.

2 In the previous edition, I used the term *Gonda-Ana*, but I have used *Garna* in this edition, a name that was used during the time of the Garna civilization, to avoid confusion with the former supercontinent Gondwana as it is called in the field of geophysics. Garna was different in size and age from Gondwana.

CHAPTER SIX

THE PATH
TO
EL CANTARE

1

Open Your Eyes

My readers, you are not beings who have been born on earth just once or twice in the past. As we have seen throughout the history of the last million years in Chapter Five, many civilizations had flourished and perished, and many continents had surfaced and then sank. Do you think those people who were born in each of those civilizations have no relationship to you whatsoever? Did those people appear out of nowhere?

The answer is no. As a matter of fact, the people who lived in each of those civilizations, the people of Atlantis or the people of Mu, were you yourselves. Deep within the soul of each of you, inside the treasure house of your memories, there is definitely a record of you being born in the past, in tens or even hundreds of civilizations. This is not something that only special kinds of people with spiritual abilities have; everyone equally has these memories of the soul. Nevertheless, people have forgotten the wisdom acquired through long years of reincarnation simply because they dwell inside a physical body.

Who you believe to be you are is not your true self; it is nothing but a costume. The physical body is just a vehicle, like a boat or a car that the soul rides to undergo training in this world. You are the captain of the boat, or the driver of the car; the boat or the car is not who you are. So now, I would like you to awaken to the other you that is controlling your physical body. I would like you to meet your true self.

If you believe you have fully understood the world with the knowledge you have acquired in one or two decades of school education, you are terribly mistaken. If you yourself neglect to explore who you truly are, who in the world would bother to tell you? To meet your true self, you need to explore on your own who this true self is.

Then, what does it mean to meet your true self? In short, it means to become aware of the truth about your soul. And to become aware of the truth about your soul, you need to explore your own mind thoroughly. If you yourself do not explore your own mind, who in the world would tell you this truth? If you yourself cannot talk about who you truly are, who in the world would talk about it for you? Being enlightened is to meet your true self. It is when you can talk about the true mind of your true self on your own. Put simply, it is to be able to confidently say, "This is me."

Human souls branched out of Buddha and are the artwork of Buddha's self-expression. However, because humans were given the freedom to create and the freedom to act, they came to live in a very selfish way, like the storied Monkey King[1]. Before long, they forgot about Buddha, the parent, forgot about the Will of Buddha, and led worldly lives full of selfish desires or worldly desires. People became really corrupted after having become more attached to this earthly world than to Heaven in the Real World. That is how a world of desire and strife was created in the other world, a world just like the earthly world, which eventually became Hell.

To know yourself means to learn that you are a child of

Buddha. It is to know the Will of Buddha. To open your eyes is to awaken to your own spirituality and to open your mind to the existence of the Real World in the fourth dimension and higher. You can choose to stay asleep if you are content with your present self and your current view of humanity. If, however, you want to open your eyes in the truest sense, you should first start by exploring your own mind. There, you will find the clues to the land of Buddha.

2

Abandon Your Attachments

To know yourself, you must get rid of yourself. In order to know your true self, you need to abandon your false self. Recognizing your false self is the first step in getting rid of it. So, let me begin by listing the types of the false self.

1. THE SELF THAT TAKES LOVE FROM OTHERS

First on the list is the self that thinks only of tearing away love from others. The Primordial Buddha gave us the universe. Human souls and human bodies were also given to us by Buddha. Buddha has given all and everything, like the sun, air, water, land, sea, animals, plants, and minerals. Even so, Buddha expects nothing in return. In this way, human beings live in a world where everything has only been given, so why is it that they think only of taking more? How much more love will satisfy them after Buddha has given so much love? Only people who are not aware of Buddha's love take the love of others. But what exactly is this love of others that they want to take? It is to get a reputation based on very worldly values.

What is the point of getting judged based on worldly values? What good does it do to get a high reputation in a third dimensional, materialistic way? How much will it help you grow? Such a mind filled with self-love will turn into a barrier between you and others, and eventually will put up wired fences all around the Earth like a zoo. Why can't you notice this? It is because you have wrong attachments. This is why you don't notice. As long as you have a mind of attachment, you cannot attain true happiness.

2. THE SELF THAT DOES NOT BELIEVE IN BUDDHA

We should feel most sorry for those who do not believe in Buddha, or those who do not believe in the world that Buddha created. These people think that humans are born by chance, as the result of copulation and that each human lives alone as a separate individual. This is the false self for whom we should feel most sorry.

"I do not believe in Buddha's salvation. If you want me to believe it, show me proof"—those who make such statements are already trying to put Buddha on trial. They have become so arrogant that they believe they have such superiority as to judge Buddha. But human beings cannot prove the existence of Buddha, who has been guiding humankind from before the birth of Earth. If they want proof, it can be shown once they die and return to the other world. But by then, it would most likely be too late. They would be in a pitch-dark world, having fallen into such a confused state that they cannot even prove their own existence.

3. THE SELF THAT MAKES NO DILIGENT EFFORTS

The third false self is the self that makes no diligent efforts. The self that makes no diligent efforts is, first, the self with a lazy mind; second, the self that neglects to study Buddha's Truth;

third, the self that does not view others fairly; and fourth, the self that is not honest, accepting or open-minded.

Buddha expects human beings to make efforts eternally. So, humans who do not make efforts shouldn't be called the children of Buddha. Are you making efforts, day by day? Are you deepening your studies of Buddha's Truth, day by day? Are you evaluating the ability and true worth of others fairly? Furthermore, are you living honestly or acceptingly? There can be no such thing as improvement or true learning of the soul for humans who are not honest, accepting or open-minded. Being of that nature is a virtue, and that in itself accords with Buddha's mind. So, if you are always contradicting others without listening to them, then it shows you are not honest, accepting or open-minded.

4. THE SELF THAT IS FULL OF ATTACHMENTS

The false self is, in short, the self that is full of attachments. To know your true self is to live day by day with Buddha's mind as your own. And to live with Buddha's mind as your own is to live day by day knowing that this world is a temporary world where you train your soul and that you must eventually let go of everything and return to the other world. No matter how much you cling on to this world, you will eventually have to leave for the other world.

Life is impermanent and you must live each day as if it were your last because you never know when you will face death. No one in Heaven is attached to this world. But everyone in Hell is attached to this world. Do not forget this fact, even for a moment.

3

Fire Up Red Like Heated Iron

Abandoning attachments is a significant decision in one's life. It is a wise decision that will guarantee happiness in your eternal life. But this does not mean that you should live passively or in a negative way at all. A positive and bold life will open up when you abandon your attachments.

Take a good look at people in the world. Do you see how weak people with attachments are? Why are they so attached to their status or reputation, or to their income in comparison to others? Why are they so obsessed over school names or company names? Why are they so concerned about trying to look good or about satisfying their vanity? What good does it do them, if any, by being attached to such things? What good will it do them, if any, by gaining the admiration of people in this world? Oh, how meaningless, how useless, and how trivial human attachments are in the eyes of the Primordial Buddha, the being that is even greater than the distant boundaries of the great universe. Can you understand this?

A true life is where you abandon all worldly attachments and fire up red and hot like heated iron. That is what we call the life as a child of Buddha. That is the kind of life Buddha appreciates.

The status, fame, or wealth that humans establish in this world cannot be taken back to the other world when they die. Any kind of worldly title obviously means nothing there. Do you know just how many people who were once known as prime ministers of Japan are now suffering in Hell? Thousands of presidents of large businesses that people envied have fallen to the Hell of Lust, the Hell of Strife, or the Hell of Beasts. Did you know about this? There were people who were good at making money who gave in to satisfying their sexual desires with women and ended their life that way. Do you know just how many hundreds of years they are suffering in Hell to compensate for mere decades of sexual pleasure? Hell is not an old story or an expedient; it actually exists. It undeniably exists at this very moment.

From the eyes of people who have mastered Buddha's Truth, the state of those suffering in Hell can be more easily seen than looking at goldfish in a fish bowl. What those in Hell have in common is that the greater attachment they have to this world, the deeper their suffering is.

The essence of humans is the mind, or the soul. The mind is everything. So, when you die, there is nothing but your own mind that you can take back with you to the other world. Only when you realize this can you, for the first time, let go and be honest. If you can only take your mind back with you, then you should at least take back a beautiful mind. Then, what is a beautiful mind like? Of course, it is a mind for which Buddha would praise you. The mind that Buddha would praise you for is a mind full of love. It is a giving mind, a nurturing mind, a forgiving mind, and a grateful mind. So, in order to take such a mind back with you, shouldn't firing up red like heated iron be all about refining and developing your mind?

What do you think is the opposite of attachment? It is love. Because love means to give. What attachments could there possibly be in the love that you continue to give for the sake of nurturing others? So, to get rid of your attachments, first start by giving love.

What have you done for your parents, who have done so much for you? What have you done for your brothers and sisters? Further, have you lived up to the expectations of your teachers who cared for you? What have you done for your friends? What have you ever done for the people who crossed paths with you in your life? What have you done for your neighbors? What have you done for your girlfriend or boyfriend? What have you done for your wife or husband? Or, how much of your parents' efforts did you remember when you raised your children? Were you able to forgive someone you resented? Have you managed to calm your angry mind? How much were you able to live up to Buddha's love as you bravely walked through your life?

4

Life Consists of Daily Challenges

Once you have let go of worldly attachments, cleared your mind, and pledged to live as a child of Buddha, what exactly should you do? It is not to retreat into the mountains, stand under a waterfall, fast, or just sit in meditation, every day. Human beings were not born to withdraw into the mountains. Human beings were not born to fast, either. You cannot attain enlightenment like that; didn't Shakyamuni Buddha of India already confirm this 2,500 years ago? In order to make use of his life, you need to realize that what leads to enlightenment is not found in such physical discipline. What truly leads to enlightenment is not found in a life that immerses the body in sensual pleasures extremely or in ascetic training that torments the body extremely. The life that Buddha expects one to live is the Middle Way that abandons these extremes in both directions.

Although the essence of human beings is the mind and the soul, this of course does not mean that you may neglect your physical body. Your physical body is a valuable vehicle received from Buddha, through your parents, for you to undergo life training. Even with objects like cars that can easily be purchased with money, there are people who love their cars and polish them every day to be spotless clean. But if people are willing to put so much energy into their cars, they should take even better care of their bodies and maintain their health by exercising appropriately and keeping in mind to eat a balanced diet. They should also get enough sleep and live orderly lives. Further, do not let your soul be controlled by alcohol because it can muddle your reasoning and intellectual ability. When people can no longer live without alcohol, they will eventually lose their reasoning ability and their bodies will become possessed by the devils of Hell; they will end up handing over their bodies. This will certainly lead to failure at work and the destruction of families.

It is easy to say that you should avoid either extreme and enter the life of the Middle Way, but it is actually very difficult to practice. The more you think about it, the more you realize how profound the Middle Way is. How, then, can you enter the life of the Middle Way? How can you obtain the yardsticks to measure it? Those are the next questions people will ask.

To enter the Middle Way, first, you need two yardsticks. One is, needless to say, the yardstick of self-reflection, which is mainly based on the Eightfold Path. The other is the yardstick of self-contemplation, mainly using the theory of the developmental stages of love. I would like you to live with these two things as your yardsticks.

The Eightfold Path teaches that you must view rightly, think rightly, speak rightly, act rightly, live rightly, make right efforts, have right will, and meditate rightly. This practice is where you find the Middle Way by correcting, in light of what is right, your thoughts and actions that have swayed to the extremes. In short, it is when you have entered the Middle Way that you will be able to live on good terms with others and live in great harmony. However, you must be aware that if you are only practicing self-reflection in light of what is right, there is a risk of your life degrading into a passive and pessimistic one. In other words, if you are too preoccupied with self-reflection, you may not be able to move forward with your life.

When you have properly reflected on yourself, the next step is to consider how to express it using your mind and through your actions. That is, through acts of gratitude. What, then, are acts of gratitude? Is it to say "thank you" to others? Sure, that is one way. But real acts of gratitude are more proactive. Real acts of gratitude are found in your answer to the question, "What have you ever done for others?"

The act is love. Love that gives. Love that you keep giving. The practice of love that expects nothing in return. This is how acts of gratitude should truly be. Therefore, from time to time, ask yourself if you are at the stage of fundamental love, forgiving love, or love incarnate. In short, you need to contemplate on your personal growth. You can accurately measure your growth by using the theory of the developmental stages of love. By doing so, you can make daily advancement.

Self-reflection and advancement—these two yardsticks represent the true life as a child of Buddha. So, you must reflect on yourself every day, refrain from extreme thoughts and actions, and contemplate on yourself every day to see if you are advancing. Only then can you say that you are winning the daily challenges of life.

5

When Life Gives Radiance

In life, you need self-reflection and advancement. However, I believe these alone do not give enough color. After all, you need radiance in life. What, then, exactly is this radiance? Let us think about this.

Radiance is a moment when light shines out its color. I believe there are three kinds of radiant moments in life. Now, let me talk about these three moments.

The first kind is when you recover from illness. Illness is indeed a time of trial in life. How you tackle this trial is a test to see the kind of person you are. Illness is a trial in two ways. One is that it comes with physical suffering. The other is that it comes with mental suffering.

First, there is the physical suffering, which is usually caused by an irregular lifestyle, overwork, or one's mistaken thoughts. So, those who suffer from illness must realize that their mind is ill, just like their body. Also, they should reflect deeply on the reason why their physical body is suffering.

We can say that up to 80 percent of people with illnesses are possessed by some kind of spirits; in many cases, the spirit of a deceased person is using the ill person's physical body and they both endure the same kind of oily sweat-soaked affliction. This is proven by how, once the possessing spirit is removed, the ill person's fever goes down immediately and he or she gets up from bed, feeling lighter in both mind and body. This shows how susceptible the human body is to spiritual influences.

What possessing spirits hate most are self-reflection and gratitude. This is because when people who are ill begin to practice self-reflection and feel gratitude, they begin to emit an aura from the back of their heads, causing them to gradually attune to different wavelengths from the possessing spirits. As a result, the spirits will no longer be able to possess them. To give out this aura even more brightly, they must solve their mental suffering.

To solve mental suffering, they first need to check the kind of attachments they have, one by one, and remove them. This may sound ironic to people who are ill, but it is only when they have removed their attachments and reached the state of mind that they are ready to die anytime, that the light of Buddha's Truth will begin to enter them with the help of their guardian and guiding spirits and they will recover rapidly from their illness. This is a miraculous moment. We can say that people who have experienced this miraculous moment of recovery from illness have gone through a great conversion and a great rebirth. What is more, this radiance is not only a light for the person, but also a light from their mind that shines upon other people.

The second kind of radiant moment is when you awaken to faith. The difference between a life without faith and a life with faith is like the difference between a person living blindly in a dark night and a person living with a lantern to light the way.

This third dimension is a world based on material things, but if your mind becomes preoccupied with material things and starts to believe that materialistic ideas are the Truth, then you will increasingly pursue physical pleasures only, or solely be caught up with strife. In short, you will become a person who has forgotten Buddha's eyes, the most pitiful state as a human. Faith is the ray of light that brightens your path at night. Only this light will enable blind humans to open their eyes to the Real World for the first time.

The third kind of radiant moment is when you receive spiritual revelations such as the phenomena of spiritual messages. The phenomena of spiritual messages are when the door of your mind opens and you become able to communicate the words of your guardian and guiding spirits in your subconscious mind.

The phenomena of spiritual channeling in a particular new psychic-based religion were nothing but spirit games played by sennins where they usually spoke nonsense and 99 percent of the channelers suffered mental breakdowns afterward. Contrary to this, the phenomena of spiritual messages at Happy Science have a distinct feature—they are phenomena involving high spirits, limited only to ones who have attained enlightenment, and the messages contain high-level Laws. Thus, as they receive teachings, they are always protected by high spirits. What is more, other people can second-handedly experience these for themselves as they study the Laws. This is a truly wonderful thing. In this way, we can say that experiencing spiritual messages from high spirits, either directly or indirectly, is the third moment of radiance in life.

6

Time of Diamond

To live your life powerfully, you need to use your limited time rightly. Human souls are reborn on earth once every hundreds or thousands of years. So, it is a very precious experience. Even so, the majority of people just spend their time idly without deeply seeking the meaning of life. What a waste. Even if, in your twilight years, you become aware of the existence of Buddha, awaken to faith and want to redo your life, you cannot get back the time already spent in this life, just like a shooting arrow or a flowing stream. So, people who have awakened to Buddha's Truth early in life should be grateful. And if they manage to live according to Buddha's Truth throughout their lives, that would be best. Of course, this is not to say that those who have encountered Buddha's Truth later in life are doomed. Even if they awaken late, their lives will become wonderful as long as they are determined enough and live in meaningful and fruitful ways.

There is a secret to life. It is to try to meditate about the moment of your death. Every now and then, try to meditate about what you will think and feel when you die. At that time, if you can think, "I'm glad to have lived" or "life is a truly wonderful thing," then it can be said you have lived a happy life. On the contrary, there are people who will have regrets welling up, one after another, as they contemplate the moment of their death. These people are to be pitied. When these people die and return to the other world, they will be made to reflect on their whole lives in front of high spirits. Their lives will be shown to them so very vividly, as if they are watching TV, in front of many others.

You will be made to see exactly what kind of person you are in the eyes of Buddha shortly after you die and return to the other world. At that time, not a single lie or excuse will help you. Then, from the looks of reaction of many others, you will realize where you should go. Those who go to Hell will choose to go to Hell themselves. This is because, once they find out the kind of person they are, they will be too ashamed to live in Heaven. In terms of physics, it means that their spiritual vibrations are coarse, so they cannot harmonize with the refined and serene vibrations of others. To put it another way, their consciousnesses have become third dimensional or materialistic and have become so "heavy" that they sink.

However, there are also people who are applauded by others when their life stories are shown in the Real World after they die. In short, when the screen shows a scene where they realize the mistakes they made in their lives, ask Buddha for forgiveness in prayer and shed tears from their eyes, those of the other world will applaud them, and tap the newly returned spirits on the shoulder to offer to shake hands. Further, when the screen shows a moment in which they stand up to devote their lives to spreading Buddha's Truth, bodhisattvas of light will rejoice in tears of delight.

I am not sure how many years or decades it will take, but this is the landscape that awaits you. The time will surely come. That is why it is important that, every now and then, you contemplate on the moment of your death, or rather, ask yourself if you are living the kind of life that leaves you with no regret even if your life were to end tomorrow. When you die, will you not be ashamed of the way you are living now? Will you have no regrets? How about in light of your conscience?

To make your time in life shine like a diamond, you need to shift your consciousness and way of thinking in this way. This means to imagine the very moment of your own death, and reflect on the way you have lived up until now. It will be as if you are practicing self-reflection from the standpoint of an impartial spectator. This is the secret to living a time of diamond. It is the secret to living a meaningful, radiant life.

7

Embrace Your Dream

In life, you need dreams. There is no hope in life without a dream. It is important that you reflect on the evil you have produced and regain good will, of course. But it wouldn't be enough to only bring your life up from negative to zero, or to break even, would it?

Embracing a dream means to plan out your life the best you can. For example, when a house is built, architects will draw up a plan that the builders use to construct a magnificent home. However, the architect of your life is no one but yourself. So, unless you come up with a beautiful design yourself, the building will be a mess. Why do you neglect to set up a plan for your own life, even though you put so much care in plan when you build your house? This is how recklessly you are living. Too many people are living life just taking everything as it comes.

Actually, making a plan for your life does not mean that you have to think so hard about it. You just need to embrace a dream and draw it. There is a huge difference in the confidence levels of living life between people with dreams and people without dreams. There is a difference in the power of persuasion between the two groups as well. When you meet people with a dream, they make you feel very happy throughout the day. You will be inspired to take on challenges and, at the same time, you will be motivated to help them achieve their dreams.

There is something about embracing a dream that fascinates people. I'm sure every single person in history who achieved something great to be passed on to future generations did not start off without a dream. Having been born as a human and living in this world, it is extremely important to think big and try to live big. Confining yourself in a small world like a bagworm does not make you humble. Humility is especially necessary when you are growing; it is precisely because you are living full of confidence that you need to stay humble. Humility, in short, acts as a brake. Yet, a car will not move forward with the brake only. What is most important for a car to move forward is the accelerator. A car cannot carry out its functions without the gas pedal. The brake is there for precaution; it is there to prevent reckless driving or an accident.

I have warned of the danger of falling to Hell on numerous occasions, but if you fear going to Hell and spend all your time chanting sutras or saying prayers every day, you will not be able to grow. So, you need to step on the gas. When you think you are going too fast, step on the brake. That is why you have the brake. But if your life is always positive, when aiming for further improvement, just make sure that your brake works properly. If you can check every day that you are immediately reflecting on your mistakes when you make them and correcting your path, then just step on the gas bravely. This is what is meant by embracing a dream and realizing it.

The effect of embracing a dream is not only that it creates a life plan; it also has a mystical function. A dream is a vision that you keep in your mind. This vision will definitely reach your guardian and guiding spirits in the other world, or the Real World. They are always looking hard for ways to protect and guide the people on earth. But wherever we go, most of the people living on earth only harbor fleeting thoughts that constantly come and go; they do not have a proper direction in life. They do not have any well-thought idea as to how they want to lead their lives.

What can guardian and guiding spirits ever do to protect and guide such people? If they teach living people all about how to live, it would deprive the people in this world of independence. The only thing that guardian and guiding spirits in the other world are allowed to do is to send inspiration to living people. Usually, this is all they can do. However, if you embrace a clear dream, your guardian and guiding spirits can just think about how you can achieve that dream and send appropriate inspiration for it. Therefore, as long as you embrace a clear dream and keep thinking about it, there is a high chance that it can come true with the help of your guardian and guiding spirits in the other world.

In truth, this is what self-realization is in the truest sense. In other words, to self-realize, first, embrace a dream. Then, visualize your dream and pray to your guardian and guiding spirits to assist you. Then, your dream will eventually take shape. This is the process. It goes without saying that the dream you embrace needs to lead to the improvement of your character and to the happiness of other people.

8

Summon Up the Golden Courage

Courage. The very sound of this word makes my heart leap, and I am sure I am not the only one. When I hear the word courage, I think of an ax cutting down a giant tree; I can almost hear the sound of those strong beats of life echoing through the forest in the early morning. This ax called courage is precisely the reason why humans can cut their way through the giant trees called difficulties in life. I think so.

Therefore, when you feel discouraged in life, I want you to remember that you have an ax of courage. When you are very miserable and dispirited, I want you to remember that Buddha has given you an ax called courage.

Human beings become spiritually blind when they are born into physical bodies; what this means is, you have to find your own way through life relying solely on your five senses. That is why Buddha gave you the ax of courage when you were born, saying, "Cut your way through the forest of destiny." Every one of you has this ax hanging on your belt. Why don't you notice it? Why do you not use your ax of courage to cut the ropes of destiny that bind you before looking to others for solutions when you suffer, or before seeking sympathy when you are in sorrow?

One of the Zen koans is a parable entitled, "The Enlightened Man." This is the 20th koan in the book titled, *The Gateless Gate,* a collection of 48 koans compiled by the Chinese Zen master, Wumen Huikai (a.k.a. Mumon Ekai, 1183 – 1260).

"Shogen asked, 'Why does the enlightened man not stand on his feet and explain himself?' And he also said, 'It is not necessary for speech to come from the tongue.'"

"Wumen's comment: Shogen spoke plainly enough, but how many will understand him? If anyone comprehends, he should come to my place, and test out my big stick. Why, look here, to test real gold you must see it through fire.

"If the feet of enlightenment moved, the great ocean would overflow; If that head bowed, it would look down upon the heavens. Such a body has no place to rest... Let another continue this poem."

The meaning of this koan can be summarized as follows:

Human beings have forgotten the immense power that is within them; they believe that they are nothing more than the materialistic physical body that could break down at any moment, as if hypnotized by worldly knowledge such as commonly accepted beliefs, public opinion and the words of doctors. However, your true self is essentially a child of Buddha with infinite power. Look, if you achieve emancipation through zen meditation, you will see your true nature, your spiritual body, become like a giant that looks down on Earth. A galaxy of this third dimensional universe ("the great ocean") is like a puddle in the higher dimensional great universe that would splash out if you stepped into it. The worlds of human enlightenment below the sixth dimension ("the heavens"), as opposed to the worlds of tathagatas and bodhisattvas, would be so far below that you will need to lower your head to see them.

It seems that Wumen Huikai had attained the enlightenment of the Tathagata Realm. When you attain the enlightenment of the Tathagata Realm, you will know that your true form is not a tiny soul dwelling in a small physical body, but an energy body extending far out into the great universe. In zen meditation, you will experience your spiritual body rapidly expanding until you can look down on the Earth far below.

Human beings essentially have such immense power; that is to say, they are beings that are completely elastic and free from any restraints. Even so, they remain bound by their own senses of the third dimensional world, by their school education, or by conventional knowledge, believing that there are no such things as spirits or the other world and restricting their freedom. And when they fall ill, they become miserable tiny beings who repeatedly say, "I don't want to die, I don't want to die."

So, bring out your golden courage, heave the golden ax and cut down the giant tree called delusion. Keep on striking powerfully with your ax. With courage, conquer your worries, sufferings, or your ties to your destiny. Then, swing your golden ax of courage and break off from the ropes of destiny that bind you.

Courage is important. It is when people summon courage that they will realize that they are the immense power. You may show your immense power at one time, rise from your sickbed and begin to live a powerful life, or be able to break off from the delusions of materialism and awaken to the Truth. Even so, you will gradually lose your willpower if you continue to receive the vibrations of this third dimensional material world and fall into temptation that third dimensional humans experience.

However, this is when you must grit your teeth and make efforts. It is like running a marathon; there will definitely be times when things get so painful that you want to give up partway. If you stop running at that time, you will definitely lose your chance of winning. This means that you will not be able to complete the race. However, once the most painful time passes, your feet will somehow feel lighter and you will be able to continue running to the end. I am sure many people have had this curious experience. The same is true for swimming. If you bear down and continue to swim without giving up, even if it becomes so hard to breathe that you want to give up, you will find that your body will become one with the water, and you can continue to swim as if you were a wave.

Of course, life is not the same as running a marathon or swimming. But similarly, there are periods in which you must persevere, no matter how hard it gets. When you manage to endure such times, you will not only gain confidence, but be able to feel Buddha's bright light close to you.

9

The Time of "Crouching Dragon": Reminiscing My Youth

Let me now talk about my personal history up till now, starting from when I was about ten years old. In the last years of elementary school, surprisingly for my age, I was able to easily endure long hours of study. As a result of my steady effort, I was able to gain an average test score of 99.7 percent throughout sixth grade. The small percentage I lost was due to careless mistakes I made on a Japanese Language and Literature test; instead of selecting the letters to multiple-choice questions, I wrote out the words and lost dozens of points.

My father took my report card with him and went to discuss my future with his acquaintance, the headmaster of a junior high school affiliated with "T" University, who then told my father that I would have no problem getting into his school. He also commented that, with my grades, I could even be accepted to Nada Junior High. But my father suggested that I go to a local junior high school, considering that I could benefit from making a lot of friends and acquaintances in my hometown in case I wanted to pursue a career in politics.

I eventually decided to take the entrance exam to enter Kawashima Junior High School in my hometown and ranked first with perfect scores. I was also the representative of the first-year students at the entrance ceremony. My good old junior high school days were the golden age for me; I served as the head of the student council, the captain of the tennis club, and the chief of the school's press committee, being in charge of editing and publishing the school newspaper. All of these experiences are the source of my leadership skills that later stood me in good stead.

My success in academic studies also continued; I kept the top position, always getting more than 50 points higher than the second place students in exams of 500 points maximum. I also ranked first on the national examinations on several occasions and astonished the teachers at my school. My homeroom teacher in my third year used to wonder, "Top students of other years often get some backlash from their peers, but you are different. For some reason, everyone listens to you; everything is decided according to what you say and everyone just follows without opposing." I remember this as if it was yesterday. I seemed to be more than just a bright student; someone with a big and profound heart and the charisma as a religious leader hidden within.

As for senior high school, I chose Tokushima Jonan High School in Tokushima City, the best school in my prefecture back in those days. Around that time, a comprehensive selection system was adopted based on the school grouping system used in Tokyo in order to prevent too many students from rural areas coming into the city. Under this system, students who scored in the top 10 percent of the entrance exam could likely attend the school of their choice, while the remaining 90 percent were likely allocated to a school based on their scores and where they lived. I was not in favor of this system allowing my school to be chosen this way, so I studied very hard. As a result, I successfully entered Tokushima Jonan High School with the highest score of those who came from rural areas. Back in those days, more than 10 students from that school would enter the University of Tokyo every year, so it was around then that I began to think more seriously about studying for the University of Tokyo.

Unfortunately, my time in senior high school was not as enjoyable as my days in junior high. I was always feeling dull and sleepy from the lack of sleep, due to the intensive kendo practices that I started and the fatigue from taking the two and a half hour-round trip commute by train between home and school. From what I remember, I only had time to study English on the dimly lit, jolting train. In the swaying carriage, I would stand with an English textbook in my right hand, an English-Japanese dictionary *Crown* in my left and a fountain pen between my fingers, tackling grammar and comprehension questions. I must have looked fierce, since I remember feeling guilty when a four-year-old girl once stood up to offer me her seat.

Although I felt I had a terribly short time to study, I always scored highest in my class. My favorite subject was Japanese Language and Literature, and in my first year of high school, I got top marks in a national distance-learning course six times in a row. This gave me a lot of confidence. As far as I know, this record still stands today. Perhaps it wasn't such a good idea to devote so much time to study Japanese Language and Literature just to get into university, but it worked to my advantage in shaping my basic skills in later years when I began a career that would require a lot of reading, writing many books, and giving talks to large audiences.

Other subjects I was also good at were Geography, Geology and Biology, although they, too, had nothing to do with my university entrance exam. Since I excelled in liberal arts subjects—English, Japanese and Social Studies—in my second year I decided to go into the science track that required me to take more Mathematics and Physics, so that I could overcome what I felt I was weak on. This was when a rumor began to spread that I might apply to Natural Sciences III (Faculty of Medicine) at the University of Tokyo, but I had already decided to apply to its Faculty of Law because it would provide me with a wider range of possibilities for my future.

In the first and second years of senior high school, I played the lead roles in school plays performed during school festivals. Although I felt offended that I was chosen against my will, perhaps I had a talent that I was unaware of, because a member of the drama club repeatedly asked me to join. Later, when I started talking in front of audiences of tens of thousands, I wished that I had joined the drama club to gain more stage experience, but by then, of course, it was too late.

In my final year of senior high, I went back to the liberal arts track for students applying to national universities. My class was of a high level; five of my classmates managed to enter Human Sciences I (Faculty of Law) and one entered Human Sciences II

(Faculty of Economics) at the University of Tokyo. Although my final academic record was not as good as I had hoped, I was glad to see that I was doing the best after entering university. As such, I successfully graduated from senior high school with the Shohaku Award, an award given to the top students.

Regarding my university entrance preparation, I took the University of Tokyo mock exam around the end of 1975, which was organized by a major cram school. The results predicted that I would be within the top 10 percent and able to enter Human Sciences I (Faculty of Law), and Human Sciences II (Faculty of Economics) or Human Sciences III (Faculty of Letters) with the best or second-best scores. I was relieved to see those results. On the actual exam which had a maximum of 440 points, I scored even higher—30 to 40 points more than I did on the mock exam—and secretly hoped that I would come within the top 10. In the spring of 1976, I successfully enrolled in the University of Tokyo, Human Sciences I.

However, my feelings soon changed to anxiety because I was surrounded by bright students from all over the country enrolled in the Faculty of Law at the University of Tokyo. I felt the need to study hard so I immersed myself in a variety of subjects, day and night, to explore the world of academia far beyond my major; I studied not only law and politics, but also sociology, history, philosophy, history of social theory, economics, management, natural sciences and international relations. I even bought books in their original language and became absorbed in them, whether they were written in English or German.

My proficiency in English was particularly high, probably because I had already acquired the top-level proficiency in national testing by the time I took the entrance exam. So, I found that I could read English much faster than the university professors and associate professors. One night, after I had casually gone to my favorite coffee shop and became absorbed in reading a 400- or 500-page book in English on European political history, I saw the owner turn away new customers at the door so that he could provide me with a quiet space to study. I remember feeling very grateful and apologetic at the same time.

But I didn't spend all my time studying. On sunny days, in the late afternoon, I used to walk around Hanegi Park near my rental room and stroll through the town of Umegaoka, sometimes jotting down verses of poetry that came to me by inspiration. I would also look to the western sky at sunset and think about the Greek philosopher Plato's philosophy on the Spirit World or Kitaro Nishida's ideas on "pure experience" and "*kensho* (seeing one's true nature)." At the time, I was already beginning to spiritually awaken to become a religious leader-to-be.

When my happy days at Komaba Campus (liberal arts courses) came to an end, I moved on to Hongo Campus (Faculty of Law). My grades remained at the top level and one of my most memorable accomplishments at the time was the research paper I wrote on political philosophy during the spring vacation of my third year. I wrote my paper on Hannah Arendt, a political philosopher in America who admired ancient Greek political thought, entitled, *On the World of Values in Hannah Arendt*. Even though her works are known to be quite difficult due to her Germanic English, I still read all her works and worked on my paper every night until six in the morning for two weeks. My friends said that my paper was too difficult to understand, but my professor praised it as a mature work, commenting that I could have a successful career as a scholar. If I were to elaborate more to make it twice as long and give it a proper introduction, he noted, it might be better than any thesis submitted by a third-year post-graduate assistant (equivalent to a doctoral dissertation). At the same time, he also expressed his concern about whether I liked studying the pragmatic law when I could think so philosophically. He asked me if I was studying enough law.

I was twenty-one years old then and was starting to show signs of an academic genius. I had a tendency to take practical subjects such as the Constitution, the Civil Code and the Penal Code lightly, being strongly attracted to metaphysics. This tendency did not change much. My professor had high expectations of me and strongly stressed that, as a law student, it was imperative that I study subjects that had practical applications in society. So, I finally became one of the people in the Hongo Campus library who thoroughly read law reports using the Japanese Compendium of Laws.

To tell the truth, I was not sure if law was a genuine academic subject. For example, I could not stop thinking about the underlying problem of the Japanese Constitution—

whether its construction and intention could be justified or not. I felt somewhat sorry for my friends who devoted themselves to memorizing the entire constitution and various theories based on it. As for the Penal Code, I could not agree with the textbook explanations of the moral basis for allowing some people to punish others, and on the definitions of crime and the criteria for judging them. I also kept wondering about the relationship between the Civil Code and Hegel's philosophy of law. The Commercial Code, which included the Companies Act, the Bills and Notes Act and the Check Act, was all too pragmatic for someone like me, who enjoyed deep philosophical contemplation.

I had similar reservations about political science. I was disappointed by the illogical explanation of a theory of political process by a professor who formed his theory using Kunio Yanagita's work on Japanese native folklore and Shichihei Yamamoto's analysis of the Japanese people. As for the international politics class, which I took out of interest, I found that, although the professor's argument against the U.S.-Japan Security Treaty based on his left-wing beliefs made sense, I felt that his conclusions were mistaken. Over a decade later, his views on the Cold War were eventually proved wrong when the Soviet Union collapsed; my intuition was right.

Thus, I was faced with the lack of, or the poorness in the depth and axiology in the studies of law and political science, and realized that there was no professor in the University of Tokyo under whom I thought it was worth studying. That being so, I had no alternative but to make my own path. I thought the only option left was to create a financial foundation and then find a way to survive until I could discover an academic subject worth studying, or if there was none, create a completely new field of my own.

Nevertheless, just before my fourth year, I decided to take the bar exam to keep my options open. At the preparatory school I attended for six months, I got top scores six times. My essays had been selected as model answers, and many people who studied them eventually passed the bar exam. As for me, although I passed the short-answer part of my exam with flying colors, exceeding the passing mark by over 10 points (out of 90 points possible), my essays did not pass, to the surprise of many of my friends. I believe this was due to the fact that I wrote the essays from a scholarly point of view, rather than a practical perspective. I was academically quite mature and had my own viewpoints. I was clearly able to point out the faults in some conventional legal theories or the accepted interpretations of case precedents. But my answers, which harshly criticized the judgment of the country's Supreme Court, had been too much for the people who graded the exams.

Nonetheless, when I discussed this later with the high spirits, I found that they had been determined to take any necessary measure to prevent me from passing the bar exam and getting a fulfilling job, so that I could give up on achieving worldly success and instead take the path to be a religious leader. So, as it turned out, I really had no chance of passing the exam.

Then, quite an unexpected path opened up before me; the person in charge of personnel at a general trading company very courteously invited me to work for them. Then, one of the company's managing directors, a graduate of my university who had later obtained an MBA from Stanford University, ardently asked me to join the company. Out of respect, I agreed to take the job.

My friends greatly criticized my decision; one of them disapproved how I turned down my professor's recommendation to enter the Bank of Japan, which was a position only available for one of his students. Someone in charge of personnel at a government-affiliated major bank suggested that I join his bank, commenting that, unlike students from other private institutions, the eventual success rate of University of Tokyo students having successfully passed the short-answer part of the bar exam while still in school was over half. To my pleasure, he also said that since I majored in political science, I would certainly pass it with top marks. His remarks indeed made sense from the fact that, although the highest scoring student on the national civil service exam for first-track candidates had entered the Ministry of Finance that year, that student had actually failed the short-answer part of the bar exam.

However, I was against the idea of relying on the power of a major institution; I rather had the impulse to pull myself up by my own bootstraps. However, doubt over the choice of my future career grew stronger, day by day, as my friend kindly warned me saying, "You don't drink, you don't play mahjong, you're not very good at socializing, and you've never been abroad. You are definitely not cut out to work at a trading company."

As graduation day approached, my love for the academic world welled up again, and I delved into books such as Carl Hilty's *Happiness* and Martin Heidegger's *Being and Time*. As I read them, I could not help but want to become a thinker, and it only grew stronger over time. I also read many books on philosophy and religion in an effort to find answers to various questions about life.

10

The Way to Enlightenment

In the soft spring sunlight on the afternoon of March 23, 1981, I was feeling very good. I was reflecting on my past, including my school days, and thinking about my future life plan. I could not hold back my desire to get out into society as an independent thinker by about the age of thirty; it felt like my calling. At the same time, I also told myself that I could not become an independent thinker without becoming financially independent first. I believed that a path would surely open before me while I made a living at the trading firm, accumulated social experiences, and deepened my own studies.

But I suddenly sensed the presence of an invisible being in my room. I was struck by a feeling that someone was trying to talk to me, so I quickly grabbed some note cards and a pencil. Then, my hand holding the pencil began to move on its own volition and wrote, *iishirase, iishirase* (Good News, Good News) on many cards. When I asked, "Who are you?" my hand signed the name "Nikko." It was the automatic writing of Nikko, one of the six senior disciples of the 13th-century Buddhist monk Nichiren.

I was surprised because I had no previous connection to the Nichiren schools of Buddhism. But since "Good News" meant "Gospel" in the Christian context, I intuitively knew that it was a moment of some kind of spiritual awakening. Above all else, I was particularly surprised to experience for myself that the other world truly did exist, as did spiritual beings, and that humans were souls with imperishable lives.

Looking back, I recalled a number of strange experiences. Perhaps because of my spiritual eye having begun to open two or three months prior to that, I had occasionally noticed a special glow in my eyes and a golden aura emitted from the back of my head. In another instance, I recalled the time when I paid a visit to a temple complex at Mount Koya when I was a student taking liberal arts courses at the university. While I was walking toward the inner sanctum, I had a vision of my future self at work using supernatural powers. Further, in the autumn of the same year, I read Masaharu Taniguchi's lecture book on *shinsokan* (literally, meditation on God) that I happened to find at a second-hand bookstore. When I tried to practice shinsokan one night, I put my hands together in prayer and felt something hot like electricity run through my hands. I was quite startled and felt strange, so I never opened the book again. At the same time, though, I also found his philosophy quite stale. I even recalled that, as I was lying in bed with a very high fever during my final years of elementary school, I had out-of-body experiences many times and traveled all the way from Heaven to the Hell of Agonizing Cries. I have been very sensitive to spiritual matters and very intuitive since birth.

The spiritual contact from Nikko in the form of automatic writing soon came to an end, and next came a spiritual communication from Nichiren. Nichiren then presented me with three words: "love, nurture, and forgive." He was probably hinting to me that I would later form the theory of the developmental stages of love. By the way, while this was happening I had been wondering if I was one of the monks affiliated with the Nichiren schools in my past life. After that, for at least a year, Nichiren made contact with me a considerable number of times, probably with the hope that I could quell the misguided religions affiliated with the Nichiren schools.

11

The Appearance of Christ and the Mission of Buddha

In June 1981, Jesus Christ came down to me and began to deliver astounding truths in a form of spiritual message. He spoke in Japanese with a bit of a foreign accent, yet his words were so sincere, powerful, and overflowing with love. My father, who was there at the time, was shocked speechless by the powerful presence of the spirit from a higher dimension. When spirits from higher dimensions are near you, you are dazzled by their brilliant light, your entire body becomes hot and you are naturally moved to tears by the shining Truth that is full of light in every word they say.

In July, the treasure house of my subconscious opened and my hidden consciousness, Gautama Siddhartha—Shakyamuni Buddha—spoke austerely and ardently on the mission of spreading Buddha's Truth, partially speaking in an ancient Indian language. He then told me that I was the spiritual being named El Cantare, the core consciousness of his soul group[2]. He also told me that El Cantare's mission is to bring salvation to all humankind through spreading Buddha's Truth, and that His roles are twofold: the role of the Amitabha (the Savior part), who represents love, mercy, and faith, and the role of the Mahavairocana (the essential part of Buddha), who represents enlightenment, spiritual discipline, and the secret doctrines of the Spirit World. El Cantare is Grand Tathagata Shakyamuni that embodies both of these; He is the Grand Savior should the first aspect be more prominent, and the Mahavairocana Buddha, the origin of the Vairocana Buddha described in the Flower Garland Sutra and Mahavairocana Sutra, should the second aspect be symbolized. Gautama Siddhartha clearly stated this.

Incredible. I was raised in a very religious family from childhood and could accept the existence of the Spirit World without question; still, I was greatly overwhelmed by the spiritual phenomenon and could not contain my surprise as to the grandness of the mission that was being told to me. What was made clear to me were these things: I am the rebirth of Buddha; with Buddha at the center, I am to put in order and unite the high spirits in the heavenly world and integrate the various religions on earth and create a new world religion; and to teach and guide people all over the world, and open a path to a new civilization. I was asked to take on a mission to open a new age.

However, I did not quit working at the trading firm just then because I wanted a little more time to explore and clarify the Spirit World and I thought I needed to undergo training as a human until I was thirty. Despite my inner conflict, however, my life in this world took a turn in the opposite direction. From 1982 to the following year, I was assigned to work at my company's New York headquarters as a trainee. So, the man who had received spiritual messages from Jesus Christ and had been told of his mission as a Buddha was working daily with people on Wall Street in the field of international finance.

After a hundred hours of private English lessons at the Berlitz language school, I passed an interview with a professor at the City University of New York, who then commented that I spoke "perfect English," and I was able to join his seminar course in international finance on the same basis as native English speakers. Together with the young business elite aged around thirty from companies such as the Bank of America, Citibank, and Merrill Lynch, I learned the concepts of foreign currency exchange. But something did not feel right. I could not bridge the gap between the reality of human society and the religious reality I was experiencing and it just kept growing wider. Back then, I would look up at the skyscraper of the World Trade Center in lower Manhattan, where I worked, and ask myself which was real—the building or the voices in my heart. My self-awareness and faith were truly tested.

When my yearlong training period was over, my unprecedented achievements were evaluated so highly that my boss offered me an expatriate staff position in New York. It was virtually an invitation to join the super elite, the best opportunity a trading company employee could dream of attaining. However, I was concerned about the manuscript of spiritual messages that I had already started to work on at the time. So, I turned down the promotion for the expatriate staff position in New York and instead invited my junior colleague to be the next trainee, as I had decided to return to Japan. It was an unusual act of selflessness and of little desire for a trading company employee, but as a religious leader, I had taken a steady step forward.

After returning to Japan, I spent two years preparing and in July 1985, I published *The Spiritual Message from Nichiren*. Later, I published other books of spiritual messages one after another; *The Spiritual Message from Kukai*, *The Spiritual Message from Jesus Christ*, *The Spiritual Message from Amaterasu-O-Mikami*, and *The Spiritual Message from Socrates*. Since I was still working for the trading firm, these books were published using my father's pen name, with my own name appearing only as a co-author.

Nonetheless, the time had finally come. In June 1986, various spirits, including Jesus Christ, came to me one after another and declared that now was the time to rise as a religious leader. In the same year, soon after my birthday on July 7, I left my company on July 15 and took my first step in the land of freedom.

At the end of August that year, I started writing *The Laws of the Sun* (the first edition) and completed it by the beginning of September. Next, in October, I began to write *The Golden Laws* (the first edition) and finished it in November. Both were published the following year and served as the driving force to launch Happy Science. The publication of my very first books on theories of the Truth rapidly attracted many members seriously seeking the Way.

12

Believe in Me and Gather to Me

The first Happy Science public lecture was held on March 8, 1987 at the Ushigome Public Hall in Tokyo. About 400 people came to hear my lecture entitled, "The Principles of Happiness." In the lecture, I proposed the four principles that constitute the basic teachings of Happy Science—the principles of love, wisdom, self-reflection, and progress—as the Principles of Happiness. I also announced the policies of Happy Science: for its foundation strategy, the first three years would be dedicated, as a study group, to setting the basis of the Laws, nurturing lecturers, and assembling methods of operating the organization; and thereafter shifting our activities to spread the Truth for major development.

In April of the same year, we started to publish our monthly magazine. The essays published in the magazine and the public lectures together set the direction and course of our future movement. Also, our seminars and training sessions produced a lot of brilliant members, and gave birth to Happy Science staff members and lecturers.

Being inspired and moved by my passionate and strong talks, participants at my public lectures kept increasing each time. In 1988, Hibiya Public Hall, which was designed to hold 2,000 people, was overflowing, and in 1989, the audience completely filled the Ryogoku Kokugikan, an indoor stadium with a capacity of 8,500. In 1990, the exhibition hall at Makuhari Messe, which holds well over 10,000 people, was filled to capacity every time I spoke there.

Then on March 7, 1991, exactly four years after my first public lecture, Happy Science was officially approved as a religious corporation, and it was the start of a new beginning. The object of worship is Grand Tathagata Shakyamuni, that is to say, El Cantare; the highest grand spirit in the ninth dimension as well as the rebirth of Buddha and the most sacred Buddha, who assumes the position of guiding even the high spirits.

In July 1991, 50,000 core believers gathered at Tokyo Dome for Goseitansai, or the Celebration of the Lord's Descent. Thus, in the very year that Happy Science was officially established as a religious corporation, it became one of the largest religious bodies in Japan, manifesting as a never-before-seen miracle in the religious world. I declared myself to be El Cantare and revealed my mission as Mahayana Buddha, or the Buddha of Salvation.

The mass media reported these facts to the whole world, bringing about the age of true religion in Japan. In the same year in September, we began the "Revolution of Hope" or our fight for justice in order to clear away the dark clouds hanging over the world of Japanese mass media and to eradicate the spiritual pollution that has continuously contaminated all Japanese people. This marked a turning point for postwar Japan toward building a Buddhaland utopia.

At the El Cantare Festival in December 1991, I made the declaration that Happy Science was in fact the number one religious organization in Japan, with more than 5.6 million followers. In 1992 and 1993, the foundation of the teachings was reinforced by Buddhist principles, and I gave many public lectures of a large scale, broadcasting them simultaneously via satellite throughout the country. At the same time, supporters of the "Revolution of Hope" continued to raise their voices all over Japan, increasing the number of our followers toward 10 million. In this way, with the tremendous victory of our "Plan Miracle," which took place from 1991 to 1993, Happy Science firmly established itself as a religious organization with faith in El Cantare at its center.

In 1994, we launched our highly anticipated "Plan Big Bang." From establishing faith to spreading the Truth: this shift in our activities was to have Happy Science take a great leap forward to become a world religion. You must proclaim the advent of Lord El Cantare and His mission to all people of the world. The supreme Buddha or the greatest Savior in the history of Earth has descended. The world is now being purified. By believing in El Cantare, humankind can be granted final, supreme, and greatest salvation.

Believe in me and gather to me—Spread this message to people all over the world. I am your Eternal Master.

ENDNOTES

1 In the classic Chinese novel *Journey to the West*, there is the Monkey King who had lived a very selfish life, but then realized that he was only a minor being compared to Buddha. (Added by translators.)

2 The reincarnations of El Cantare are as follows: 1) Ra Mu (Mu Continent), 2) Thoth (Atlantis Continent), 3) Rient Arl Croud (ancient Incan Empire), 4) Ophealis (Greece), 5) Hermes (Greece), 6) Gautama Siddhartha (India), and 7) Ryuho Okawa (Japan). In principle, the El Cantare consciousness consists of ninth dimensional soul siblings.

Afterword

For now, I believe, this book has successfully revealed the framework of the philosophy of Buddha's Truth that Happy Science is spreading, as well as its purpose and mission. This is the one and only book in the entire world that clearly describes Creation, the stages of love, the structure of enlightenment and the transition of civilizations, as well as the true mission of El Cantare.

You should believe this book, for you will read it as the Buddhist scripture, or the Bible, later on in your future lives.

For a deeper understanding of this book, it is worth noting that while the first edition described the Spirit World simply as a dichotomy between Heaven and Hell, this edition further explains that Heaven also consists of the front side and the rear side. I have also removed many parts that were written from the perspective of the rear side, including the descriptions of the Spirit World, sets of values, and historical views. So, I believe it is much more logically clear now. Similarly, while I used the word *God* throughout the first edition, I preferred to replace it with the word *Buddha* in this book because this is more accurate as the basic philosophies of Buddha. Further, I have replaced some religious terms that were unique to Happy Science with commonly accepted terms such as *arhat* because I thought it necessary as we become a major religion. This is out of courtesy, so that the readers of this book, which will certainly sell more than a million copies, can read it more easily.

For my readers who find it hard to understand the entire scope of the basic teachings of Happy Science from this book, I am planning to write a new book on the theory of the Truth. Stay tuned.

Ryuho Okawa
Master and CEO of Happy Science Group
June 1994

ABOUT THE AUTHOR

Founder and CEO of Happy Science Group.

Ryuho Okawa was born on July 7th 1956, in Tokushima, Japan. After graduating from the University of Tokyo with a law degree, he joined a Tokyo-based trading company. While working at its New York headquarters, he studied international finance at the Graduate Center of the City University of New York. In 1981, he attained Great Enlightenment and became aware that he is El Cantare with a mission to bring salvation to all humankind.

In 1986, he established Happy Science. It now has members in 169 countries across the world, with more than 700 branches and temples as well as 10,000 missionary houses around the world.

He has given over 3,500 lectures (of which more than 150 are in English) and published over 3,150 books (of which more than 600 are Spiritual Interview Series), and many of which are translated into 42 languages. Along with *The Laws of the Sun* and *The Laws of Hell*, many of the books have become best sellers or million sellers. To date, Happy Science has produced 27 movies under the supervision of Okawa. He has given the original story and concept and is also the Executive Producer. He has also composed music and written lyrics of over 450 pieces.

Moreover, he is the Founder of Happy Science University and Happy Science Academy (Junior and Senior High School), Founder and President of the Happiness Realization Party, Founder and Honorary Headmaster of Happy Science Institute of Government and Management, Founder of IRH Press Co., Ltd., and the Chairperson of NEW STAR PRODUCTION Co., Ltd. and ARI Production Co., Ltd.

BOOKS BY RYUHO OKAWA

El Cantare Trilogy

The first three volumes of the Laws Series, *The Laws of the Sun* (this book), *The Golden Laws*, and *The Laws of Eternity* make a trilogy that completes the basic framework of the teachings of God's Truths. The Laws of the Sun discusses the structure of God's Laws, *The Golden Laws* expounds on the doctrine of time, and *The Laws of Eternity* reveals the nature of space.

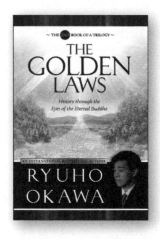

The Golden Laws

History through the Eyes of
the Eternal Buddha

E-book • 204 pages • $13.99
ISBN: 978-1-941779-82-8 (Sep. 24, 2015)

Throughout history, Great Guiding Spirits of Light have been present on Earth in both the East and the West at crucial points in human history to further our spiritual development. *The Golden Laws* reveals how Divine Plan has been unfolding on Earth, and outlines 5,000 years of the secret history of humankind. Once we understand the true course of history, through past, present and into the future, we cannot help but become aware of the significance of our spiritual mission in the present age.

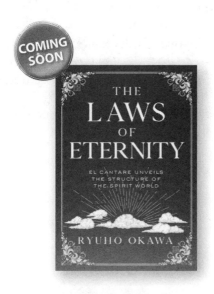

The Laws of Eternity

El Cantare Unveils the Structure of the Spirit World

Paperback • 200 pages • $17.95
ISBN: 978-1-958655-16-0 (May 15, 2024)

"Where do we come from and where do we go after death?"

This unparalleled book offers us complete answers to life's most important questions that we all are confronted with at some point or another.

In *The Laws of Eternity*, author Ryuho Okawa takes us on a journey to the other world, a place where we came from before we were born and return to after death.

The other world has a multidimensional structure consisting of the worlds of the fourth, fifth, sixth, seventh, eighth, and ninth dimensions, where souls with the same level of spiritual awareness and similar characteristics reside.

This book reveals the eternal mysteries and the ultimate secrets of Earth's spirit group that have been covered by the veil of legends and myths. Encountering the long-hidden Eternal Truths that are revealed for the first time in human history will change the way you live your life now.

Latest Laws Series

The Laws Series is an annual volume of books that are comprised of Ryuho Okawa's core teachings that function as universal guidance to all people. They are of various topics that were given in accordance with the changes that each year brings. *The Laws of the Sun* (this book), the first publication of the laws series, ranked in the annual best-selling list in Japan in 1994. Since, the laws series' titles have ranked in the annual best-selling list for more than two decades, setting socio-cultural trends in Japan and around the world.

The Laws of Hell

"IT" follows.....

Paperback • 264 pages • $17.95
ISBN: 978-1-958655-04-7 (May 1, 2023)

Whether you believe it or not, the Spirit World and hell do exist. Currently, the Earth's population has exceeded 8 billion, and unfortunately, 1 in 2 people are falling to hell.

This book is a must-read at a time like this since more and more people are unknowingly heading to hell; the truth is, new areas of hell are being created, such as 'internet hell' and 'hell on earth.' Also, due to the widespread materialism, there is a sharp rise in the earthbound spirits wandering around Earth because they have no clue about the Spirit World. To stop hell from spreading and to save the souls of all human beings, Ryuho Okawa has compiled vital teachings in this book.

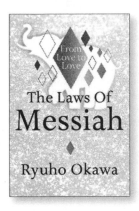

The Laws Of Messiah

From Love to Love

Paperback • 248 pages • $16.95
ISBN: 978-1-942125-90-7 (Jan. 31, 2022)

"What is Messiah?" This book carries an important message of love and guidance to people living now from the Modern-Day Messiah or the Modern-Day Savior. It also reveals the secret of Shambhala, the spiritual center of Earth, as well as the truth that this spiritual center is currently in danger of perishing and what we can do to protect this sacred place.

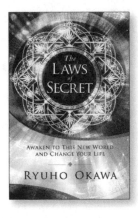

The Laws of Secret

Awaken to This New World
and Change Your Life

Paperback • 248 pages • $16.95
ISBN:978-1-942125-81-5 (Apr. 20, 2021)

Our physical world coexists with the multi-dimensional spirit world and we are constantly interacting with some kind of spiritual energy, whether positive or negative, without consciously realizing it. This book reveals how our lives are affected by invisible influences, including the spiritual reasons behind influenza, the novel coronavirus infection, and other illnesses. The new view of the world in this book will inspire you to change your life in a better direction, and to become someone who can give hope and courage to others in this age of confusion.

Other Books

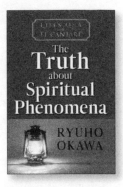

The Truth about Spiritual Phenomena
Life's Q&A With El Cantare

Paperback • 232 pages • $17.95
ISBN: 978-1-958655-0-92 (Oct. 27, 2023)

These are the records of Ryuho Okawa's answers to 26 questions related to spiritual phenomena and mental health, which were conducted live during his early public lectures with the audience. With his great spiritual ability, he revealed the unknown spiritual Truth behind the spiritual phenomena.

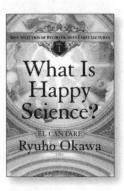

What Is Happy Science?
Best Selection of Ryuho Okawa's Early Lectures (Volume 1)

Paperback • 256 pages • $17.95
ISBN: 978-1-942125-99-0 (Aug. 25, 2023)

The Best Selection series is a collection of Ryuho Okawa's passionate lectures during the ages of 32 to 33 that reveal the mission and goal of Happy Science. This book contains the eternal Truth, including the meaning of life, the secret of the mind, the true meaning of love, the mystery of the universe, and how to end hatred and world conflicts.

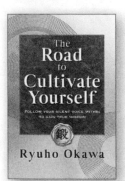

The Road to Cultivate Yourself
Follow Your Silent Voice Within to Gain True Wisdom

Paperback • 256 pages • $17.95
ISBN: 978-1-958655-05-4 (Jun. 22, 2023)

In the age of uncertainty, how should we live our lives?

This book offers unchanging Truth in the ever-changing world, such as the secrets to become more aware about the spiritual self and how to increase intellectual productivity amidst the rapid changes of the modern age. It is packed with Ryuho Okawa's crystallized wisdom of life.

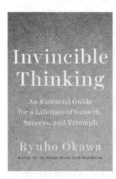

Invincible Thinking

An Essential Guide for a Lifetime of Growth, Success, and Triumph

Hardcover • 208 pages • $16.95
ISBN: 978-1-942125-25-9 (Sep. 5, 2017)

When we encounter adversity, hardship or failure, how can we find the resilience and will to persevere? On the other hand, what can we do when everything is going well for us?

In this book, Ryuho Okawa lays out the principles of invincible thinking that will allow us to achieve long-lasting triumph. This powerful and unique philosophy is not only about becoming successful or achieving our goal in life, but also about building the foundation of life that becomes the basis of our life-long, lasting success and happiness.

The Strong Mind

The Art of Building the Inner Strength to Overcome Life's Difficulties

Paperback • 192 pages • $15.95
ISBN: 978-1-942125-36-5 (May 25, 2018)

The strong mind is what we need to rise time and again, and to move forward no matter what difficulties we face in life.

In this book, Ryuho Okawa presents a self-transformative perspective on life's hardships and challenges as precious opportunities for inner growth. It will inspire and empower you to take courage, develop a mature and cultivated heart, and achieve resilience and hardiness so that you can break through the barriers of your limits. With this book as your guide, life's challenges will become treasures that bring lasting and continuous enrichment to your soul.

The Laws of Success

A Spiritual Guide to Turning
Your Hopes Into Reality

Paperback • 208 pages • $15.95
ISBN: 978-1-942125-15-0 (Mar. 15, 2017)

The Laws of Success offers 8 spiritual
principles that, when put to practice in
our day-to-day life, will help us attain
lasting success. The timeless wisdom and
practical steps that Ryuho Okawa offers
will guide us through any difficulties and
problems we may face in life, and serve
as guiding principles for living a positive,
constructive, and meaningful life.

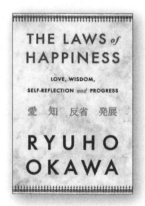

The Laws of Happiness

Love, Wisdom, Self-Reflection and
Progress

Paperback • 264 pages • $16.95
ISBN: 978-1-942125-70-9 (Aug. 28, 2020)

Happiness is not found outside us; it is
found within us. It is in how we think, how
we look at our lives, and how we devote
our hearts to the work we do. Discover
how the Fourfold Path of Love, Wisdom,
Self-Reflection and Progress creates a life
of sustainable happiness.

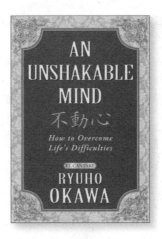

An Unshakable Mind

How to Overcome Life's Difficulties

Paperback • 180 pages • $17.95
ISBN:978-1-942125-91-4 (Nov. 30, 2023)

Do you have "an unshakable mind?"

This book will guide you to build the genuine self-confidence necessary to shape a resilient character and withstand life's turbulence.

Author Ryuho Okawa breaks down the cause of life's difficulties and provides solutions to overcome them from the spiritual viewpoint of life based on the laws of the mind.

As you engage further with this book, you will discover the hidden spiritual causes behind some of life's difficulties. Finding the true causes of problems makes it easier to confront, tackle and solve them.

This practical yet very insightful book is filled with powerful words of encouragement that will resonate within your soul. Let this book be your companion through life's hardships.

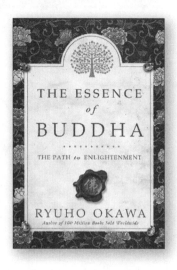

The Essence of Buddha

The Path to Enlightenment

Paperback • 208 pages • $14.95
ISBN: 978-1-942125-06-8 (Oct. 1, 2016)

In this book, Ryuho Okawa imparts in simple and accessible language his wisdom about the essence of Shakyamuni Buddha's philosophy of life and enlightenment–teachings that have been inspiring people all over the world for over 2,500 years. By offering a new perspective on core Buddhist thoughts that have long been cloaked in mystique, Okawa brings these teachings to life for modern people. *The Essence of Buddha* distills a way of life that anyone can practice to achieve a life of self-growth, compassionate living, and true happiness.

The True Eightfold Path

Guideposts for Self-Innovation

Paperback • 256 pages • $16.95
ISBN: 978-1-942125-80-8 (Mar. 30, 2021)

This book explains how we can apply the Eightfold Path, one of the main pillars of Shakyamuni Buddha's teachings, as everyday guideposts in the modern-age to achieve self-innovation to live better and make positive changes in these uncertain times.

The Rebirth of Buddha

My Eternal Disciples, Hear My Words

Paperback • 280 pages • $17.95
ISBN: 978-1-942125-95-2 (Jul. 15, 2022)

These are the messages of Buddha who has returned to this modern age as promised to his eternal beloved disciples. They are in simple words and poetic style, yet contain profound messages. Once you start reading these passages, you will remember why you chose to be born in the same era as Buddha. Listen to the voices of your Eternal Master and awaken to your calling.

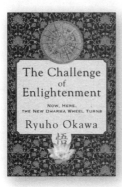

The Challenge of Enlightenment

Now, Here, the New Dharma Wheel Turns

Paperback • 380 pages • $17.95
ISBN: 978-1-942125-92-1 (Dec. 20, 2022)

Buddha's teachings, a reflection of his eternal wisdom, are like a bamboo pole used to change the course of your boat in the rapid stream of the great river called life. By reading this book, your mind becomes clearer, learns to savor inner peace, and it will empower you to make profound life improvements.

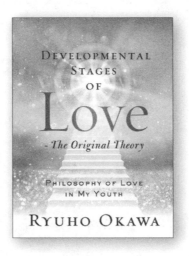

Developmental Stages of Love
- The Original Theory

Philosophy of Love in My Youth

Hardcover • 200 pages • $17.95
ISBN: 978-1-942125-94-5 (Jun. 15, 2022)

This book is about author Ryuho Okawa's original philosophy of love which serves as the foundation of love in the chapter three of *The Laws of the Sun*. It consists of series of short essays authored during his age of 25 through 28 while he was working as a young promising business elite at an international trading company after attaining the Great Enlightenment in 1981. This revolutionary philosophy, developmental states of love, is the idea to unite love and enlightenment, West and East, and bridges Christianity and Buddhism. It is also the starting point of the global utopian movement, Happy Science.

The Ten Principles from El Cantare Volume I

Ryuho Okawa's First Lectures on His Basic Teachings

Paperback • 232 pages • $16.95
ISBN: 978-1-942125-85-3 (Dec. 15, 2021)

This book contains the historic lectures given on the first five principles of the Ten Principles of Happy Science from the author, Ryuho Okawa, who is revered as World Teacher. These lectures produced an enthusiastic fellowship in Happy Science Japan and became the foundation of the current global utopian movement. You can learn the essence of Okawa's teachings and the secret behind the rapid growth of the Happy Science movement in simple language.

The Ten Principles from El Cantare Volume II

Ryuho Okawa's First Lectures on His Wish to Save the World

Paperback • 216 pages • $16.95
ISBN: 978-1-942125-86-0 (May. 3, 2022)

A sequel to *The Ten Principles from El Cantare Volume I*. Volume II reveals the Creator's three major inventions; the secret of the creation of human souls, the meaning of time, and 'happiness' as life's purpose. By reading this book, you can not only improve yourself but learn how to make differences in society and create an ideal, utopian world.

A NEW GENRE OF SPIRITUAL MYSTERY NOVELS
- The Unknown Stigma Trilogy -

The Unknown Stigma 1
\<The Mystery\>

Hardcover • 192 pages • $17.95
ISBN: 978-1-942125-28-0 (Oct. 1, 2022)

The first spiritual mystery novel by Ryuho Okawa. It happened one early summer afternoon, in a densely wooded park in Tokyo: following a loud scream of a young woman, the alleged victim was found lying with his eyes rolled back and foaming at the mouth. But there was no sign of forced trauma, nor even a drop of blood. Then, similar murder cases continued one after another without any clues. Later, this mysterious serial murder case leads back to a young Catholic nun...

The Unknown Stigma 2
<The Resurrection>

Hardcover • 180 pages • $17.95
ISBN: 978-1-942125-31-0 (Nov. 1, 2022)

A sequel to *The Unknown Stigma 1 <The Mystery>* by Ryuho Okawa. After an extraordinary spiritual experience, a young, mysterious Catholic nun is now endowed with a new, noble mission. What kind of destiny will she face? Will it be hope or despair that awaits her? The story develops into a turn of events that no one could ever have anticipated. Are you ready to embrace its shocking ending?

The Unknown Stigma 3
<The Universe>

Hardcover • 184 pages • $17.95
ISBN: 978-1-958655-00-9 (Dec. 1, 2022)

In this astonishing sequel to the first two installments of *The Unknown Stigma*, the protagonist journeys through the universe and encounters a mystical world unknown to humankind. Discover what awaits her beyond this mysterious world.

Words of Wisdom Series

Words for Life

Paperback • 136 pages • $15.95
ISBN: 979-8-88737-089-7 (Mar. 16, 2023)

Ryuho Okawa has written over 3,150 books on various topics. To help readers find the teachings that are beneficial for them out of the extensive teachings, the author has written 100 phrases and put them together. Inside you will find words of wisdom that will help you improve your mindset and lead you to live a meaningful and happy life.

Words for Building Character

Paperback • 140 pages • $15.95
ISBN: 979-8-88737-091-0 (Jun. 21, 2023)

When your life comes to an end, what you can bring with you to the other world is your enlightenment, in other words, the character that you build in this lifetime. If you can read, relish, and truly understand the meaning of these religious phrases, you will be able to attain happiness that transcends this world and the next.

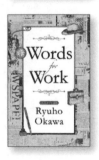

Words for Work

Paperback • 140 pages • $15.95
ISBN: 979-8-88737-090-3 (Jul. 20, 2023)

Through his personal experiences at work, Okawa has created these phrases regarding philosophies and practical wisdom about work. This book will be of great use to you throughout your career. Every day you can contemplate and gain tips on how to better your work as well as to deepen your insight into company management.

Words to Read in Times of Illness

Hardcover • 136 pages • $17.95
ISBN: 978-1-958655-07-8 (Sep. 15, 2023)

Ryuho Okawa has written 100 Healing Messages to comfort the souls of those going through any illness. When we are ill, it is an ideal time for us to contemplate recent and past events, as well as our relationship with people around us. It is a chance for us to take inventory of our emotions and thoughts.

Other Recommended Titles

THE UNHAPPINESS SYNDROME
28 Habits of Unhappy People (and How to Change Them)

THE STARTING POINT OF HAPPINESS
An Inspiring Guide to Positive Living with Faith,
Love, and Courage

THE MIRACLE OF MEDITATION
Opening Your Life to Peace, Joy, and the Power Within

THE ROYAL ROAD OF LIFE
Beginning Your Path of Inner Peace, Virtue, and
a Life of Purpose

TWICEBORN
My Early Thoughts that Revealed My True Mission

THE NEW RESURRECTION
My Miraculous Story of Overcoming Illness and Death

SPIRITUAL WORLD 101
A Guide to a Spiritually Happy Life

THE CHALLENGE OF THE MIND
An Essential Guide to Buddha's Teachings:
Zen, Karma, and Enlightenment

THE POWER OF BASICS
Introduction to Modern Zen Life
of Calm, Spirituality and Success

For a complete list of books, visit okawabooks.com

MUSIC BY RYUHO OKAWA

El Cantare Ryuho Okawa Original Songs

A song celebrating Lord God / With Savior

Words & Music by Ryuho Okawa

1. A song celebrating Lord God—Renewal ver.
2. With Savior —Renewal ver.
3. A song celebrating Lord God— Renewal ver. (Instrumental)
4. With Savior —Renewal ver. (Instrumental)
5. With Savior —Renewal ver. (Instrumental with chorus)

The Water Revolution

English and Chinese version

For the truth and happiness of the 1.4 billion people in China who have no freedom. Love, justice, and sacred rage of God are on this melody that will give you courage to fight to bring peace.

The Thunder

a composition for repelling the Coronavirus

We have been granted this music from our Lord. It will repel away the novel Coronavirus originated in China. Experience this magnificent powerful music.

Listen now today!

WHO IS EL CANTARE?

El Cantare means "the Light of the Earth." He is the Supreme God of the Earth who has been guiding humankind since the beginning of Genesis, and He is the Creator of the universe. He is whom Jesus called Father and Muhammad called Allah, and is *Ame-no-Mioya-Gami*, Japanese Father God. Different parts of El Cantare's core consciousness have descended to Earth in the past, once as Alpha and another as Elohim. His branch spirits, such as Shakyamuni Buddha and Hermes, have descended to Earth many times and helped to flourish many civilizations. To unite various religions and to integrate various fields of study in order to build a new civilization on Earth, a part of the core consciousness has descended to Earth as Master Ryuho Okawa.

Alpha is a part of the core consciousness of El Cantare who descended to Earth around 330 million years ago. Alpha preached Earth's Truths to harmonize and unify Earth-born humans and space people who came from other planets.

Elohim is a part of the core consciousness of El Cantare who descended to Earth around 150 million years ago. He gave wisdom, mainly on the differences of light and darkness, good and evil.

Ame-no-Mioya-Gami (Japanese Father God) is the Creator God and the Father God who appears in the ancient literature, *Hotsuma Tsutae*. It is believed that He descended on the foothills of Mt. Fuji about 30,000 years ago and built the Fuji dynasty, which is the root of the Japanese civilization. With justice as the central pillar, Ame-no-Mioya-Gami's teachings spread to ancient civilizations of other countries in the world.

Shakyamuni Buddha was born as a prince into the Shakya Clan in India around 2,600 years ago. When he was 29 years old, he renounced the world and sought enlightenment. He later attained Great Enlightenment and founded Buddhism.

Hermes is one of the 12 Olympian gods in Greek mythology, but the spiritual Truth is that he taught the teachings of love and progress around 4,300 years ago that became the origin of the current Western civilization. He is a hero that truly existed.

Ophealis was born in Greece around 6,500 years ago and was the leader who took an expedition to as far as Egypt. He is the God of miracles, prosperity, and arts, and is known as Osiris in the Egyptian mythology.

Rient Arl Croud was born as a king of the ancient Incan Empire around 7,000 years ago and taught about the mysteries of the mind. In the heavenly world, he is responsible for the interactions that take place between various planets.

Thoth was an almighty leader who built the golden age of the Atlantic civilization around 12,000 years ago. In the Egyptian mythology, he is known as God Thoth.

Ra Mu was a leader who built the golden age of the civilization of Mu around 17,000 years ago. As a religious leader and a politician, he ruled by uniting religion and politics.

ABOUT HAPPY SCIENCE

Happy Science is a religious group founded on the faith in El Cantare who is the God of the Earth, and the Creator of the universe. The essence of human beings is the soul that was created by God, and we all are children of God. God is our true parent, so in our souls we have a fundamental desire to "believe in God, love God, and get closer to God." And, we can get closer to God by living with God's Will as our own. In Happy Science, we call this the "Exploration of Right Mind." More specifically, it means to practice the Fourfold Path, which consists of "Love, Wisdom, Self-Reflection, and Progress."

Love: Love means "love that gives," or mercy. God hopes for the happiness of all people. Therefore, living with God's Will as our own means to start by practicing "love that gives."

Wisdom: By studying and putting spiritual knowledge into practice, you can cultivate wisdom and become better at resolving problems in life.

Self-Reflection: Once you learn the heart of God and the difference between His mind and yours, you should strive to bring your own mind closer to the mind of God—that process is called self-reflection. Self-reflection also includes meditation and prayer.

Progress: Since God hopes for the happiness of all people, you should also make progress in your love, and make an effort to realize utopia in which everyone in your society, country, and eventually all humankind can become happy.

As we practice this Fourfold Path, our souls will advance toward God step by step. That is when we can attain real happiness— our souls' desire to get closer to God comes true.

In Happy Science, we conduct activities to make ourselves happy through belief in Lord El Cantare, and to spread this faith to the world and bring happiness to all. We welcome you to join our activities!

We hold events and activities to help you practice the Fourfold Path at our branches, temples, missionary centers and missionary houses

Love: We hold various volunteering activities. Our members conduct missionary work together as the greatest practice of love.

Wisdom: We offer our comprehensive books collection, many of which are available online and at Happy Science locations. In addition, we give out numerous opportunities such as seminars or book clubs to learn the Truth.

Self-Reflection: We offer opportunities to polish your mind through self-reflection, meditation, and prayer. There are many cases in which members have experienced improvement in their human relationships by changing their own minds.

Progress: We also offer seminars to enhance your power of influence. Because it is also important to do well at work to make society better, we hold seminars to improve your work and management skills.

"The True Words Spoken By Buddha"

The True Words Spoken By Buddha is an English sutra given directly from the spirit of Shakyamuni Buddha, who is a part of Master Ryuho Okawa's subconscious. The words in this sutra are not of a mere human being but are the words of God or Buddha sent directly from the ninth dimension, which is the highest realm of the Earth's Spirit World.

The True Words Spoken By Buddha is an essential sutra for us to connect and live with God or Buddha's Will as our own.

MEMBERSHIPS

MEMBERSHIP

If you would like to know more about Happy Science, please consider becoming a member. Those who pledge to believe in Lord El Cantare and wish to learn more can join us.

When you become a member, you will receive the following sutra books: *The True Words Spoken By Buddha*, *Prayer to the Lord* and *Prayer to Guardian and Guiding Spirits*.

DEVOTEE MEMBER

If you would like to learn the teachings of Happy Science and walk the path of faith, become a Devotee member who pledges devotion to the Three Treasures, which are Buddha, Dharma, and Sangha. Buddha refers to Lord El Cantare, Master Ryuho Okawa. Dharma refers to Master Ryuho Okawa's teachings. Sangha refers to Happy Science. Devoting to the Three Treasures will let your Buddha nature shine, and you will enter the path to attain true freedom of the mind.

Becoming a devotee means you become Buddha's disciple. You will discipline your mind and act to bring happiness to society.

✉ EMAIL OR ☎ PHONE CALL
Please see the contact information page.

🔊 ONLINE [member.happy-science.org/signup/ 🔍]

CONTACT INFORMATION

Happy Science is a worldwide organization with branches and temples around the globe. For a comprehensive list, visit the worldwide directory at happy-science.org. The following are some of our main Happy Science locations:

UNITED STATES AND CANADA

New York
79 Franklin St., New York, NY 10013, USA
Phone: 1-212-343-7972
Fax: 1-212-343-7973
Email: ny@happy-science.org
Website: happyscience-usa.org

New Jersey
66 Hudson St., #2R, Hoboken, NJ 07030, USA
Phone: 1-201-313-0127
Email: nj@happy-science.org
Website: happyscience-usa.org

Chicago
2300 Barrington Rd., Suite #400,
Hoffman Estates, IL 60169, USA
Phone: 1-630-937-3077
Email: chicago@happy-science.org
Website: happyscience-usa.org

Florida
5208 8th St., Zephyrhills, FL 33542, USA
Phone: 1-813-715-0000
Fax: 1-813-715-0010
Email: florida@happy-science.org
Website: happyscience-usa.org

Atlanta
1874 Piedmont Ave., NE Suite 360-C
Atlanta, GA 30324, USA
Phone: 1-404-892-7770
Email: atlanta@happy-science.org
Website: happyscience-usa.org

San Francisco
525 Clinton St.
Redwood City, CA 94062, USA
Phone & Fax: 1-650-363-2777
Email: sf@happy-science.org
Website: happyscience-usa.org

Los Angeles
1590 E. Del Mar Blvd., Pasadena,
CA 91106, USA
Phone: 1-626-395-7775
Fax: 1-626-395-7776
Email: la@happy-science.org
Website: happyscience-usa.org

Orange County
16541 Gothard St. Suite 104
Huntington Beach, CA 92647
Phone: 1-714-659-1501
Email: oc@happy-science.org
Website: happyscience-usa.org

San Diego
7841 Balboa Ave. Suite #202
San Diego, CA 92111, USA
Phone: 1-626-395-7775
Fax: 1-626-395-7776
E-mail: sandiego@happy-science.org
Website: happyscience-usa.org

Hawaii
Phone: 1-808-591-9772
Fax: 1-808-591-9776
Email: hi@happy-science.org
Website: happyscience-usa.org

Kauai
3343 Kanakolu Street, Suite 5
Lihue, HI 96766, USA
Phone: 1-808-822-7007
Fax: 1-808-822-6007
Email: kauai-hi@happy-science.org
Website: happyscience-usa.org

Toronto

845 The Queensway
Etobicoke, ON M8Z 1N6, Canada
Phone: 1-416-901-3747
Email: toronto@happy-science.org
Website: happy-science.ca

Vancouver

#201-2607 East 49th Avenue,
Vancouver, BC, V5S 1J9, Canada
Phone: 1-604-437-7735
Fax: 1-604-437-7764
Email: vancouver@happy-science.org
Website: happy-science.ca

INTERNATIONAL

Tokyo

1-6-7 Togoshi, Shinagawa,
Tokyo, 142-0041, Japan
Phone: 81-3-6384-5770
Fax: 81-3-6384-5776
Email: tokyo@happy-science.org
Website: happy-science.org

London

3 Margaret St.
London, W1W 8RE United Kingdom
Phone: 44-20-7323-9255
Fax: 44-20-7323-9344
Email: eu@happy-science.org
Website: www.happyscience-uk.org

Sydney

516 Pacific Highway, Lane Cove North,
2066 NSW, Australia
Phone: 61-2-9411-2877
Fax: 61-2-9411-2822
Email: sydney@happy-science.org

Sao Paulo

Rua. Domingos de Morais 1154,
Vila Mariana, Sao Paulo SP
CEP 04010-100, Brazil
Phone: 55-11-5088-3800
Email: sp@happy-science.org
Website: happyscience.com.br

Jundiai

Rua Congo, 447, Jd. Bonfiglioli
Jundiai-CEP, 13207-340, Brazil
Phone: 55-11-4587-5952
Email: jundiai@happy-science.org

Seoul

74, Sadang-ro 27-gil,
Dongjak-gu, Seoul, Korea
Phone: 82-2-3478-8777
Fax: 82-2-3478-9777
Email: korea@happy-science.org

Taipei

No. 89, Lane 155, Dunhua N. Road,
Songshan District, Taipei City 105, Taiwan
Phone: 886-2-2719-9377
Fax: 886-2-2719-5570
Email: taiwan@happy-science.org

Taichung

No. 146, Minzu Rd., Central Dist.,
Taichung City 400001, Taiwan
Phone: 886-4-22233777
Email: taichung@happy-science.org

Kuala Lumpur

No 22A, Block 2, Jalil Link Jalan Jalil Jaya
2, Bukit Jalil 57000,
Kuala Lumpur, Malaysia
Phone: 60-3-8998-7877
Fax: 60-3-8998-7977
Email: malaysia@happy-science.org
Website: happyscience.org.my

Kathmandu

Kathmandu Metropolitan City,
Ward No. 15, Ring Road, Kimdol,
Sitapaila Kathmandu, Nepal
Phone: 977-1-537-2931
Email: nepal@happy-science.org

Kampala

Plot 877 Rubaga Road, Kampala
P.O. Box 34130 Kampala, UGANDA
Email: uganda@happy-science.org

ABOUT HAPPINESS REALIZATION PARTY

The Happiness Realization Party (HRP) was founded in May 2009 by Master Ryuho Okawa as part of the Happy Science Group. HRP strives to improve the Japanese society, based on three basic political principles of "freedom, democracy, and faith," and let Japan promote individual and public happiness from Asia to the world as a leader nation.

1) Diplomacy and Security: Protecting Freedom, Democracy, and Faith of Japan and the World from China's Totalitarianism

Japan's current defense system is insufficient against China's expanding hegemony and the threat of North Korea's nuclear missiles. Japan, as the leader of Asia, must strengthen its defense power and promote strategic diplomacy together with the nations which share the values of freedom, democracy, and faith. Further, HRP aims to realize world peace under the leadership of Japan, the nation with the spirit of religious tolerance.

2) Economy: Early economic recovery through utilizing the "wisdom of the private sector"

Economy has been damaged severely since the outbreak of the novel coronavirus originated in China. Many companies have been forced into bankruptcy or out of business. What is needed for economic recovery now is not subsidies and regulations by the government, but policies which can utilize the "wisdom of the private sector."

For more information, visit en.hr-party.jp

HAPPY SCIENCE ACADEMY JUNIOR AND SENIOR HIGH SCHOOL

Happy Science Academy Junior and Senior High School is a boarding school founded with the goal of educating the future leaders of the world who can have a big vision, persevere, and take on new challenges.

Currently, there are two campuses in Japan; the Nasu Main Campus in Tochigi Prefecture, founded in 2010, and the Kansai Campus in Shiga Prefecture, founded in 2013.

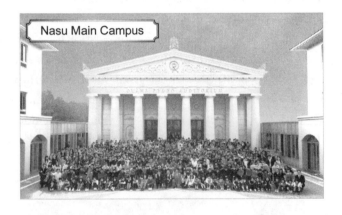

Nasu Main Campus

Kansai Campus

HSU HAPPY SCIENCE UNIVERSITY

THE FOUNDING SPIRIT AND THE GOAL OF EDUCATION

Based on the founding philosophy of the university, "Exploration of happiness and the creation of a new civilization," education, research and studies will be provided to help students acquire deep understanding grounded in religious belief and advanced expertise with the objectives of producing "great talents of virtue" who can contribute in a broad-ranging way to serve Japan and the international society.

FACULTIES

Faculty of human happiness

Students in this faculty will pursue liberal arts from various perspectives with a multidisciplinary approach, explore and envision an ideal state of human beings and society.

Faculty of successful management

This faculty aims to realize successful management that helps organizations to create value and wealth for society and to contribute to the happiness and the development of management and employees as well as society as a whole.

Faculty of future creation

Students in this faculty study subjects such as political science, journalism, performing arts and artistic expression, and explore and present new political and cultural models based on truth, goodness and beauty.

Faculty of future industry

This faculty aims to nurture engineers who can resolve various issues facing modern civilization from a technological standpoint and contribute to the creation of new industries of the future.

ABOUT IRH PRESS USA INC.

Founded in 2013, New York based IRH Press USA, Inc. is the North American affiliate of IRH Press Co., Ltd., Japan. The Press exclusively publishes comprehensive titles on Spiritual Truth, religious enrichment, Buddhism, personal growth, and contemporary commentary by Ryuho Okawa, the author of more than 3,150 unique publications, with hundreds of millions of copies sold worldwide. For more information, visit Okawabooks.com.

Follow us on:

f Facebook: Okawa Books   **◎** Instagram: OkawaBooks

▶ Youtube: Okawa Books   **🐦** Twitter: Okawa Books

P Pinterest: Okawa Books   **g** Goodreads: Ryuho Okawa

——— **NEWSLETTER** ———

To receive book related news, promotions and events, please subscribe to our newsletter below.

⚭ irhpress.com/pages/subscribe

——— **AUDIO / VISUAL MEDIA** ———

YOUTUBE   **PODCAST**

Introduction of Ryuho Okawa's titles; topics ranging from self-help, current affairs, spirituality, religion, and the universe.